BEGINNER'S GUIDE TO
COLOURWORK
Knitting

16 projects and techniques
to learn to knit with colour

Ella Austin

www.sewandso.co.uk

BEGINNER'S GUIDE TO
COLOURWORK
Knitting

16 projects and techniques
to learn to knit with colour

Ella Austin

Contents

Introduction

For me, colour is the most exciting part of knitting! Cables, lace, texture, and beautiful shaping certainly have their appeal, but it's colour that makes me smile and gets me eager to cast something on.

I've found that many knitters who feel the same excitement about colourwork knitting also feel apprehensive. Firstly, there are the colourwork techniques to learn, and they can appear complicated. Secondly, and often the biggest obstacle, is the task of finding colours that 'work' together.

The first concern is easiest to overcome; colour techniques may look impressive, but they're almost always deceptively easy to knit! Just take it stitch by stitch and you'll be fine.

The second issue is more complex. This book will give advice on colour choices, as well as a few 'ground rules' that are helpful to bear in mind. However, the most important advice is to simply try things out. You might even surprise yourself! Try not to be disheartened when something doesn't 'work' like you want it to. Remember with knitting, you can simply unpick your stitches, refine your colour options and try again – persistence is the key to colour happiness.

This book is written as a colourwork knitting course that intertwines the teaching of the techniques with the projects. Each design includes advice on yarn and colour choices as well as step-by-step tutorials for the specific methods required. I believe that this approach is more helpful to the learner as it combines the theory of the technique with a practical example.

Of course, you can also refer to the tutorials individually and apply them to different projects. Likewise, the projects are accessible to experienced knitters who would simply like to make the designs.

I hope you enjoy learning new techniques and playing with colour!

Ella

Choosing Colours

Colour can be very personal as we all have our own perceptions and tastes. We may already have favourite colours and palettes that we are drawn to. However, choosing colours to combine for a colourwork project can offer its own challenges! Sometimes it's as simple as picking a bunch of colours that you love, other times more thought should be given to the attributes of the colour.

Attributes of Colour

Colour theory usually refers to three main attributes – Hue, Value and Saturation.

- **Hue** – describes the pure colour itself, e.g. green. When we describe a colour, e.g. light green or grass green, green is the hue. Basic colour wheels show the hues.

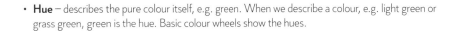

- **Value** – describes how light or dark the colour is, e.g. yellow is lighter than purple. Value is the most important attribute to consider for colourwork knitting. A strong contrast between light and dark will enhance the knitted patterns.

Low value   High value

- **Saturation** – describes the intensity of the colour. A pure hue such as red can be mixed with white, grey or black to affect the saturation. Using lots of saturated colours can make a project look vivid and bold whereas undersaturated colours will look subtler. Mixing saturated colours with undersaturated colours can be very effective.

Undersaturated   Very saturated

Hue

This colour wheel shows the primary, secondary and tertiary colours. Red, yellow and blue are the three primary colours. All other colours can be made by mixing combinations of these three colours.

The colour wheel can be split in half with those closest to orange being described as 'warm' and those closest to blue being 'cool'. Warm colours seem to stand out while cool colours seem to recede. With this in mind it can sometimes be effective to pick warm colours for parts of a pattern that you would like to stand out and cool colours as background colours.

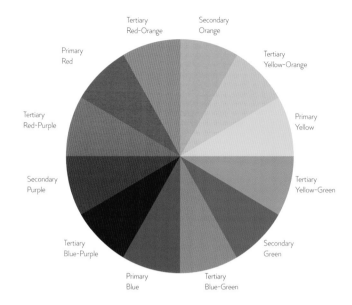

Value

Value refers to contrast; how light or dark a colour is. Value is very important to consider in colourwork knitting, particularly stranded knitting. For a stranded colourwork pattern to be intelligible there needs to be a high contrast between the two colours used together.

It can be surprisingly hard to determine value by looking at two colours together. Red and green, for example, can be very close in value despite looking distinct as two different colours. It can be helpful to take a black and white photograph of your yarn choices (or use software to make a colour photograph appear greyscale) to determine the colour values and whether there is enough contrast for the affect that you are aiming for.

A colour's value can be affected by its saturation. Red, for example, can be light or dark. Each different hue has a value range.

Colour *Value* *Value Range*

Saturation

Saturation refers to the purity of a colour's hue. The intensity of the colour can be affected by adding white, grey or black.

- Tint – mixes a colour with white.
- Tone – mixes a colour with grey.
- Shade – mixes a colour with black.

The saturation can affect the colour's value. Mixing a hue with white makes the colour lighter and mixing with black makes it darker.

Picking lots of saturated colours from all around the colour wheel will result in a project that is bright and bold, which might be considered by some as loud or garish. I find that it's most effective to limit saturated colours and use them alongside light, dark or toned colours. Using similar hues but with varied saturation is also very effective. The Thorn Stitch Shawl pattern in this book uses a dark pink-purple with a very light purple-pink.

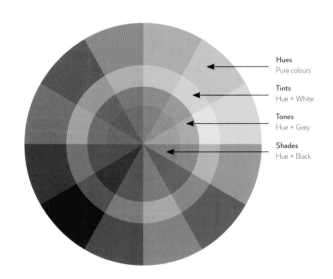

Colour Inspiration

Colour inspiration can be found everywhere and in many different ways. Colour wheels can be helpful and colour palette suggestions can be found in design books, magazines and online. Sometimes you can be struck by a colour combination that you happen to notice – this could be anything from a painting you love or a view from your window to wallpaper patterns, book covers and even food.

Whether you are searching for colour combinations or just happen to notice them, it's a good idea to start collecting inspiration in notebooks, files, folders, image sharing websites, and wherever you can. Save images that you find online, grab a camera if needed, jot down notes, record ideas and keep it all somewhere that you can refer back to. Once you have chosen the colours that you would like to use, you can search for yarns.

Yarn Colours

Yarn is available in a huge range of colours. There are natural undyed colours, solid dyed colours, and multicoloured yarns that are dyed and spun in a variety of techniques.

Most colourwork techniques work well with yarns that are dyed in a single solid colour. However, multicoloured yarns, variegated, tonal and semi-solid coloured yarns can be beautiful and so much fun to knit with! Some techniques suit these yarns more than others. It depends on the colourwork design that you are knitting and how much the patterning of the yarn colours will obscure the effect of the knitted colourwork pattern.

Stripes, intarsia and modular designs can be very effective with multicoloured yarns and can even enhance the pattern, whereas it's a good idea to be more cautious when using them for slipped stitch and stranded patterns. Knitting a swatch is the best way to see how your chosen yarn colours will work with the stitch pattern for your project.

Swatching Colours

Knitting a swatch is usually recommended when starting a new project so that you can check your tension. It's also important for finding out how ideas work in practice. Some colours look great together but might not suit a certain design when they're knitted up together. This is particularly true if the colours are too close in value for a detailed pattern to be clear. Other colour combinations might not be to your usual taste but end up working well in a pattern. When unexpected colour combinations work well, the results can look distinctive and impressive.

Experienced designers will usually have tried many colour combinations before finding something that works, so don't be disheartened if the colours you've chosen don't look right the first time. An advantage of knitting is that you can simply unpick and try again. Keep refining your colour options and eventually you'll find the perfect combination for your project.

To knit a swatch you should cast on at least 10cm (4in) worth of stitches. The number of stitches and rows needed to make a 10cm (4in) square will be given at the beginning of each pattern, in the tension information. If using a stitch pattern, it will also help to cast on a multiple of the stitches needed for the pattern repeat. You can often find this number on the pattern chart or by counting the number of stitches in a repeat section of the pattern.

Using the Graphic Hat project as an example, I cast on 40 stitches for a swatch. This number is more than the 24 stitches that should make 10cm (4in) of fabric and is a multiple of 8, which is the number of stitches that the pattern repeat is worked across.

In order to test your tension accurately, make sure that you swatch with the same method as your project – if your project is knitted flat, then your swatch should be knitted flat; if your project is knitted in the round, then your swatch should be knitted in the round.

The Graphic Hat swatches below were knitted in the round, then cut open to make them easier to measure and view. I did this by joining my 40 stitches in the round and knitting a small tube in the stitch pattern. I followed the chart using my chosen colours and then cast off all but the last 8 stitches. I dropped the last 8 stitches, allowing them to unravel down to the the cast-on edge, then I cut theses strands of yarn and blocked the swatches. As I don't need the ends to be secure, I didn't reinforce or knot them.

Knitting a swatch flat is an easier process. Simply work your swatch until it's at least 10cm (4in) long and cast off.

For some knitters, swatching can feel like a bit of chore, but knitting swatches to try out yarns, colours and stitch patterns can be great fun. The process is similar to an artist sketching.

Yarn and Tools

Knitting Needles

Knitting needles come in a variety of sizes and styles and are made from different materials. Usually knitters find their own preferences and I think it's a good idea to try different styles to find your own favourites. It's well worth investing in good quality tools that feel comfortable to you and enhance your enjoyment of knitting.

When choosing the right needle for a design, the important thing to take note of is the size of your knitting needle in terms of its circumference. These are usually marked on the needle in millimetres (mm) or UK or US sizes. If you're unsure, then use a needle gauge to check your size. Generally, as far as metric and US needle sizes are concerned, larger needle sizes are used for knitting thicker yarns and smaller sizes for thinner yarns. You can use the table below for needle size conversions, if needed.

UK	Metric	US
14	2mm	0
13	2.25mm	1
-	2.5mm	1.5
12	2.75mm	2
11	3mm	-
10	3.25mm	3
-	3.5mm	4
9	3.75mm	5
8	4mm	6
7	4.5mm	7
6	5mm	8
5	5.5mm	9
4	6mm	10
3	6.5mm	10.5
2	7mm	10.75
1	7.5mm	-
0	8mm	11
00	9mm	13
000	10mm	15
-	12mm	17
-	15mm	19
-	20mm	36
-	25mm	50

Some knitting patterns can be knitted on straight needles, but others are worked in the round and these require either double-pointed needles (DPNS) or circular needles.

- Straight needles – Needles with one pointed end to make new stitches and a knob at the other end to prevent stitches falling off. These come in different lengths.

- Double-pointed needles (DPNS) – As the name suggests, these are knitting needles with points at each end of the needle. Although they come in different lengths they tend to be significantly shorter than straight needles and usually come in sets of four or five needles. They are used to work small circumferences in the round, such as socks or mitts. DPNS can appear daunting as the knitted fabric is attached to at least three needles – and the idea of knitting with that many needles at once is unfathomable! It's important to remember that the knitter will only be working with two of the needles at any given time and the remaining needles are simply 'holding' the stitches until you work around to them.

- Circular needles – Circulars are composed of two straight needles joined by a flexible cable. The needles have pointed tips and are usually 10-15cm/4-6in long. The length of the cord can vary from about 23cm/9in to 150cm/60in. Circular needles can be used for straight knitting as well as circular knitting.

For my own knitting toolkit I like to use 80cm/32in metal circular needles with sharp tips for pretty much everything, whether I'm working on flat knitting, or circular. I use the 'magic loop' technique for knitting small circumferences.

Other Tools and Accessories

No special tools are required for colourwork knitting – your usual knitting toolkit should be sufficient for colourwork knitting too! A full list of tools for each project is listed at the beginning of the pattern. However, the following items may also be useful.

- Needle gauge – If you need to check the circumference of your knitting needles.

- Stitch holder – Stitch holders are like long safety pins that can be used for holding stitches securely. Personally, I prefer to use scrap yarn to hold stitches as I find it less cumbersome when attached to my work and scrap yarn has greater flexibility.

- Scrap yarn – My stitch holder of choice! I also use scrap yarn to make markers by knotting a small loop in a contrasting colour to my work. I keep small lengths of scrap sock yarn in my knitting toolkit – this will also be used for reinforcing knitting when steeking stranded knitting.

- Crochet hook – Crochet hooks are handy in knitting kits. Some knitters like to use them to pick up dropped stitches. They can be used to make fringes on the ends of scarfs. In this book we use a crochet hook for reinforcing knitting when steeking and for a bit of optional crochet – just a very simple chain stitch to make a button loop.

- Needle – A large blunt-ended needle such as a tapestry/wool needle is essential for weaving in ends and sewing parts together if required.

- Scissors – Most knitters like these small and sharp. These are particularly important for steeking. Other yarn cutters can be used for cutting yarns but I just stick with scissors.

- Measuring tape – For measuring! I like a retractable one to keep my toolkit tidy.

- Markers – These are little loops or hoops that are placed on the needle between two stitches to mark a place in the pattern. You can get all different types, including some very pretty ones!

- Row counter – There are many different types of row counters: digital counters, little barrel counters that can be attached to knitting needles, pendant counters, beaded counters, counting apps for smart phones and tablets. Personally, I keep a written tally using a pencil on a notepad or the margin of my printed pattern.

- Blocking equipment – Blocking wires or pins can be used to help shape knitting that is being blocked into shape. These are most often useful for shawls, where stretching out the knitting can have a great effect on the finished item. Blocking mats can be used for pinning knitting to – or your knitting can be pinned out over a mattress. Also for blocking, I use a wash basin or large bowl to immerse my knitting, and a large towel to absorb some of the water and for drying the knitting on.

- Bobbins – Bobbins are the only toolkit item specific to colourwork knitting. They are most useful for intarsia projects that use lots of small amounts of different colours. You can buy knitting bobbins, or you can make them from cardboard, or improvise with pegs or clips. Alternatively, you can knit intarsia without bobbins and just wind off small balls from the main ball of yarn.

- Pompom makers – These handy tools make easy work of creating pompoms. Alternatively, you can use cardboard cut into circles.

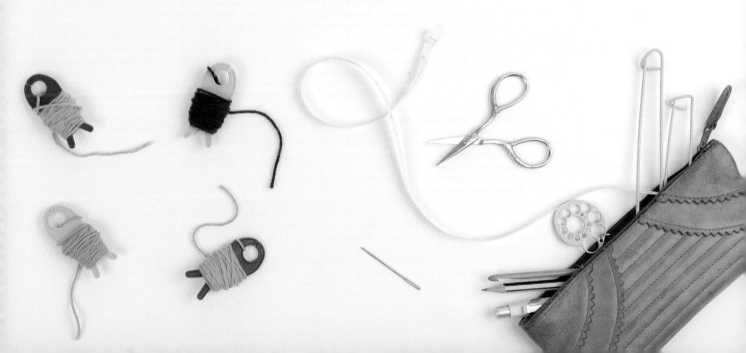

Yarn

Knitters love yarn! We get excited by the possibilities. I look at a ball of yarn and I see a whole myriad of things I want to knit with it. However, with experience and study I've got better at understanding which yarns best suit certain projects for the results I want.

When we talk about yarn, the most important things to think about are yarn weight and yarn fibre.

Yarn Weight

This refers to the thickness of the yarn. Thinner yarn produces a thinner fabric and usually takes longer to knit. You can use the table below for yarn weight conversions, if needed.

UK	US
2ply	Lace weight
4ply	Fingering/sock weight
DK light	Sport weight
Double knitting	Light worsted
Aran	Worsted/fisherman/medium
Chunky	Bulky
Super chunky	Super bulky

- 2ply/lace weight – A very thin light yarn, perfect for delicate shawls, and often used for lace knitting. The needle size used with this yarn will vary depending on how light and open you would like your fabric to be.

- 4ply/fingering/sock weight – Sometimes called 4ply, although the 'ply' of yarn is really the number of strands that it is composed of. This yarn weight is usually the thinnest yarn that we use for colourwork knitting. It's ideal for socks and mitts as the knitted fabric is quite light and flexible. It's also great for hats, scarfs, shawls, garments, toys, just about anything really. Needle sizes for this yarn usually vary between 2.25mm-3.25mm.

- DK light/sport weight – Slightly thicker than 4ply yarn and slightly thinner than double knitting (DK). Usually calls for needle sizes between 2.75mm-4mm.

- Double knitting (DK)/light worsted – Lots of knitters favour this weight yarn as it knits up into a medium weight fabric that is easy to wear. Needle sizes for this yarn usually fall between 3.5mm-4.5mm.

- Aran/worsted/fisherman/medium – Aran is a little thicker than worsted but they are similar in weight and knit up a thick and cosy fabric. Usually calls for needle sizes between 4.5mm-6mm.

- Chunky/bulky – This yarn choice is ideal for quick knits. Needles sizes are usually between 6mm-8mm.

- Super chunky/super bulky – Like chunky/bulky yarn, only even thicker. These yarns are usually knitted with needle sizes over 8mm up to 15mm, or sometimes even bigger.

Yarn is usually sold in balls or skeins that weigh 25g, 50g or 100g. Bear in mind that thicker yarns will have less metreage/yardage than thinner yarns per gram. For example a 100g skein of DK/light worsted yarn will be a much longer length of yarn than a 100g skein of chunky/bulky yarn.

Generally you will need to buy more balls or skeins of thicker yarns to finish a project compared to thinner yarns.

Yarn bought in skeins will need to be wound into a ball or 'yarn cake'. You can do this by hand, or by using a yarn swift and ball winder.

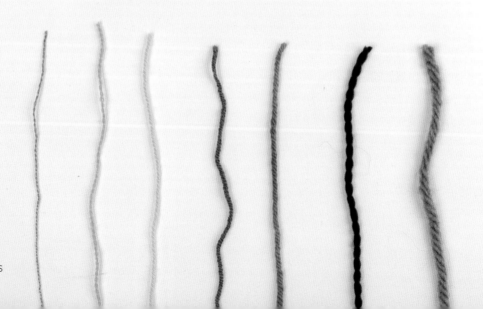

Yarn Fibre

This is the content of the yarn, or what it is made from. Some yarns are made from one material and others are blends combining the qualities from a range of materials.

- Synthetic fibres – Acrylic and polyester are synthetic fibres that are strong, easy to wash and usually relatively inexpensive. Acrylic is a good choice for blankets, making them easier to care for and, as a large project, more affordable to make. Many sock yarns contain a percentage of nylon to make hand-knitted socks more durable.

- Animal fibres – Wool, alpaca, mohair and silk are just some of the animal fibres you can knit with. Some of these yarns are very luxurious, and some, such as silk, can get quite expensive. Animal fibres have insulating properties that make them ideal for warm and cosy knits. They also have a range of other benefits such as being more breathable and odour-resistant. Lots of knitters favour wool because it creates a tactile fabric that enhances stitch definition and colourwork. Natural fibres also block out beautifully and maintain their shape really well.

- Plant fibres – Cotton, bamboo and linen are natural plant-fibres that are soft and cool to wear. Plant fibres knit up into a drapey fabric and are great for loose garments as well as homewares. Projects made from plant fibres are usually easy to wash and care for.

All of these fibres have their own unique qualities and benefits. Different treatment processes, spinning methods and blending of fibres can have a big effect on a yarn. Yarn made from one fibre can be very different from another of the same type. Using wool as an example, superwash Merino is a highly processed soft and smooth wool that feels and acts very differently to a woollen spun Shetland wool, which is fuzzy with a more natural-feeling finish.

Substituting Yarn

Most patterns will suggest a specific yarn for a design, and the sample will be knitted in that yarn. That doesn't mean that you have to use the same yarn. Sometimes the suggested yarn might have been discontinued or might not be easily available. In any case it's often preferable to substitute for a yarn that suits your own taste, needs and budget.

When substituting yarns, it's often a good idea to ensure that your yarn is a similar weight to the recommended yarn and that it has similar qualities.

Reading Charts

Colourwork knitting patterns often include charts, sometimes alongside written instructions, and sometimes in place of written instructions. As colourwork knitting is very visual, charts are often the clearest way to communicate the directions.

Charts are made from a grid of squares and each square represents an action. The action may require you to work one stitch or more. The chart key (sometimes called a legend) will explain what the action should be.

Charts are usually numbered along the bottom and along one side or both sides. Numbers across the bottom represent the stitches. The numbers along the side or sides represent rows if you are knitting flat, or rounds if you are knitting in the round. If you're knitting a pattern flat in rows, then each row of the chart will be read following the direction of your knitting, so from right to left for the first row, then from left to right for the second row, and so on, working back and forth. If you're working in the round, then the chart will be read from right to left for all rounds. Charts are always read from the bottom up.

Charts often represent only a small part of the knitting and are intended to be repeated across the knitted work. Sometimes only a part of the chart will be repeated. This will be marked out on the chart as a repeat area and may have a bold outline around the stitches to be repeated. Otherwise the key or instructions will indicate the stitches to be repeated.

Simple Charts

This simple colourwork chart form the Monochrome Mitts pattern is read from right to left for every round. Every stitch will be knitted and the colours of the grid squares indicate which colour yarn to use. The chart repeat is 4 stitches and these are repeated across the round a number of times.

For this pattern, on Round 1 you will read the first row of the chart. Two stitches are knitted using Yarn B, then two stitches are knitted using Yarn C. This 4-stitch chart pattern is repeated across the same row of knitting until you reach the end of the round. For the next round you will read the second row of the chart, and so on. After a few rounds this will become intuitive, particularly as the knitting will closely resemble the chart visually.

Mitts Chart

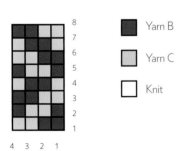

■ Yarn B

▢ Yarn C

□ Knit

Complex Charts

The chart below from the Thorn Stitch Shawl pattern is one of the most complex in this book. The chart is shaped, rather than rectangular, due to the shaping worked within the pattern. It is numbered up both sides as it is worked flat in rows. It is not numbered along the bottom because there are different numbers of stitches required due to the increase on each row. It's a slipped stitch pattern chart and the column on the right indicates the colour to be used for each row. Over the pattern of the chart, the slipped stitch squares are filled with the same colour as the row that the stitch is slipped up from. This gives a clearer visual representation of what the stitches will look like along the needle and over the knitted fabric. The chart also features 'no stitch' squares and a repeat section indicated by the thick red outline. The 'no stitch' squares are there simply to balance the shape of the chart around the increase and decrease areas. The repeat section shows the stitches of the pattern that will be repeated along the row.

All of these details may seem daunting at first but, as with every chart, if you just focus on the next stitch to be worked you will find that it's easier to knit than it looks!

To begin working the pattern from the chart, work the first row from right to left, indicated by the placement of the row number. You will be using Yarn A, indicated by the yarn colour column to the right of the chart. Begin by purling a stitch, then purling another stitch, then working a yarn over (YO) and then knitting the next stitch. Next the pattern repeat begins, which is highlighted by the red box. For the pattern repeat, first skip the 'no stitch' square and move to the next square across. Work a KYOK, which is K1, YO, K1 all into the next stitch (to increase 2 stitches). Then skip the next 'no stitch' square and knit the next 3 stitches. Note that for the first few rows, the pattern repeat area is only worked once. When you work the same rows later on they will be repeated more times until there are 2 stitches remaining before the first marker. After the pattern repeat, skipping the 'no stitch' squares, work KYOK into the next stitch, then knit the last stitch before the marker. Moving on to the central three stitches of the chart, make 1 stitch before the marker (to increase), then knit the central stitch. Continue to follow the chart pattern for the second half of the stitches, which is a mirror image of the first half.

Shawl Chart

Column on the right shows the colour of yarn in use for the row

	Yarn A		Knit on RS, purl on WS	⊻	KYOK	⊼	Knit 2 together
	Yarn B	•	Purl	⊬	Slip stitch purlwise	ML	M1L
	No stitch (move on to next instruction)	○	Yarn over	⋋	Slip, slip, knit	MR	M1R
	Pattern repeat area						

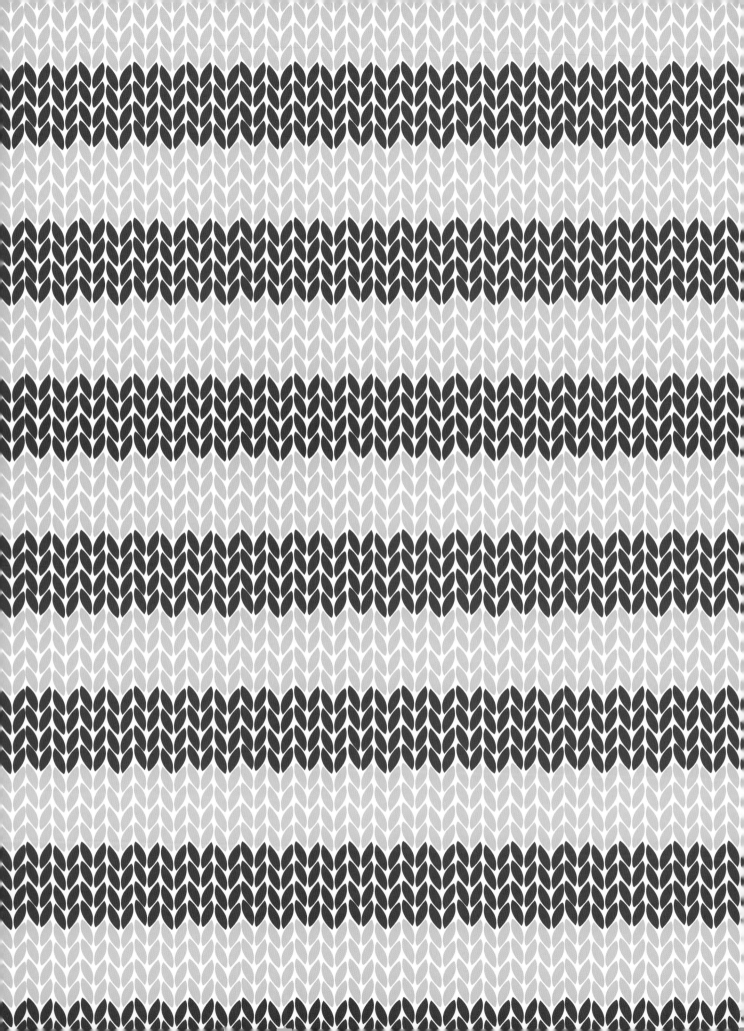

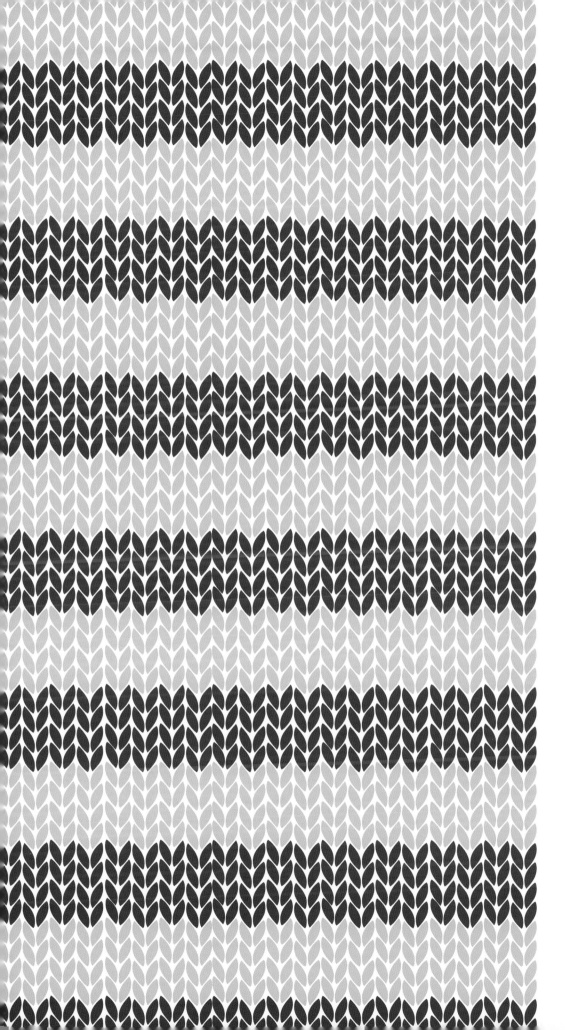

Stripes

Marled Scarf

A simple garter stitch scarf is always a good place to start! This classic hand-knit offers the perfect introduction to playing with colour. This scarf is knitted using two strands of yarn held together, so you can experiment with blending different colours as well as striping them alongside each other. I've chosen five colours from all around the colour wheel, avoiding the bright hues, and I've included three monochrome colours. Where I've knitted solid-coloured stripes I've kept these stripes narrow for a subtle accent.

You will need

Yarn

Drops Alpaca Sport (100% alpaca), 166m/182yds per 50g ball, in the following shades:

+ **Yarn A:** Aqua Grey Mix (7323); 1 ball
+ **Yarn B:** Dark Grey Mix (0506); 1 ball
+ **Yarn C:** Light Grey Mix (0501); 1 ball
+ **Yarn D:** Goldenrod (2923); 1 ball
+ **Yarn E:** Off White (0100); 1 ball
+ **Yarn F:** Maroon Mix (3650); 1 ball
+ **Yarn G:** Turquoise (2917); 1 ball
+ **Yarn H:** Light Pink (3140); 1 ball

Needles and Accessories

+ Pair of 5mm (US 8/UK 6) needles or size needed to achieve correct tension

Size

One size: 152 x 18cm/60 x 7in

Skills

Casting on, knit, working with two yarns together as one strand, casting off

Tension

16 sts and 28 rows to 10 x 10cm/4 x 4in over garter stitch, using 5mm needles, after washing and blocking

Pattern

Yarn(s)	No. of rows
D	12
B & E	18
F	4
C & G	12
B & H	22
C	8
D & E	16
C & F	12
B	2
A	6
A & H	14
D	4
B & G	16
B & E	26
F	6
A	26
B & C	12
D	8
B & E	18
F	4
C & G	12
C & E	6
B & H	22
C	8
D & E	16
C & F	12
B	4
A	6
A & H	14
D	4
B & G	16
C & E	26
F	6
A	14
C & D	8
B & C	20
H	4
C	6
B & F	10
C & G	18
D	4
B & E	24
F	6
A	18
B & C	30

Using two strands of **Yarn A**, cast on 30 sts.

Row 1 (RS): K.

Row 2 (WS): K.

Rows 3-28: K 26 rows.

Switch to one strand of **Yarn B** and one strand of **Yarn C** held together (see Tutorial 1: Changing colour).

Row 1: K.

Rows 2-12: K 11 rows.

Continue working in this way, holding two strands of yarn together and knitting every row (garter stitch) and following the sequence of colours shown in the table. Always change colour after working a wrong side row.

Cast off.

Finishing

- Block scarf carefully (see Finishing: Blocking) and note that alpaca can be very delicate when wet. Lift your knitting carefully out of the water after blocking and ensure that you dry the scarf flat without stretching it.

- Weave in all ends (see Tutorial 2: Weaving in ends on garter stitch).

Note

When using one colour, hold two strands of the same colour together. You can take one strand from the centre of the ball and one from the outside of the ball. Alternatively split your yarn into two balls before you begin.

Tutorial 1: Changing colour

When knitting patterns say 'Switch to **Yarn B**', it really is as easy as it sounds! For this Marled Scarf pattern we are using two strands of yarn at once but the instructions are exactly the same.

1. Drop the yarn that you have finished knitting with and leave it hanging by the side. Cut the yarn from the ball, leaving an end (or yarn tail) of about 15cm/6in to weave in at the end.

2. Pick up the new colour, also leaving a tail of 15cm/6in to weave in at the end.

3. Knit the first stitch (images 1 and 2). This stitch will look loose when you first knit it, but that's normal. Gently pulling the yarn tails of both colours will neaten the end stitches a little as you work, and once you weave the ends in the stitches will even out and look tidy.

4. Continue knitting with your new colour (image 3).

Tutorial 2: Weaving in ends on garter stitch

When knitting colourwork there can be lots of ends to weave in, so it's a good idea to make sure that those ends are being dealt with in a way that is both neat and secure. My preferred technique for weaving in ends is similar to a duplicate stitch technique. Where possible, always weave in ends against the matching colour.

1. Ensure that the 'wrong side' of your work is facing. Thread your loose end onto a needle. Run the needle under the closest purl bump.

2. Take your needle through your knitting and run your needle under the 'v' shape in the row below, still following the same length of yarn in the knitted fabric.

3. Insert your needle back into the purl bump that you last came through and bring the yarn through.

4. Turn your needle and, following the st underneath your yarn, run the needle under the next purl bump.

5. Continue in this way, following the path of the knitted yarn on the fabric until you have woven in at least 5 sts. Cut yarn.

Chevron Blanket

With the addition of some simple shaping, stripes can become chevrons! This throw is an ideal relaxing knit and a great opportunity to play about with colour combinations. It's easy to customise this design by changing the thickness of the stripes or by using a different number of colours. I had so much fun picking out colours for this design! I used a painting full of vibrant, saturated hues as inspiration and found similar bright colours in a hand-dyed yarn. I striped the yarns somewhat randomly, with the aim of keeping an even balance of light/dark and warm/cool colours.

You will need

Yarn

Malabrigo Rios (90% merino wool, 10% nylon), 400m/437yds per 100g skein, in the following shades:

- **Yarn A:** Fresco Y Seco (128); 1 skein
- **Yarn B:** Frank Ochre (035); 1 skein
- **Yarn C:** English Rose (057); 1 skein
- **Yarn D:** Sabiduria (136); 1 skein
- **Yarn E:** Reflecting Pool (133); 1 skein
- **Yarn F:** Water Green (083); 1 skein
- **Yarn G:** Glitter (048); 1 skein
- **Yarn H:** Lettuce (037); 1 skein
- **Yarn I:** Ravelry Red (611); 1 skein

Needles and Accessories

- Pair of 5mm (US 8/UK 6) needles or size needed to achieve correct tension

Size

One size: 86 x 124cm/34 x 49in

Skills

Casting on, knit, purl, increasing, decreasing, casting off

Tension

17 sts and 24 rows to 10 x 10cm/4 x 4in over st st, using 5mm needles, after washing and blocking

Pattern

Using **Yarn A**, cast on 181 sts.

Garter Stitch Edge

Row 1 (WS): K.

Row 2 (RS): K2, (k1, m1L, k6, CDD, k6, m1R) to last 3 sts, k3.

Rows 3-4: Repeat last 2 rows once more.

Row 5: K.

Blanket

Switch to **Yarn B** (see Tutorial 1: Changing colour).

Row 1 (RS): K2, (k1, m1L, k6, CDD, k6, m1R) to last 3 sts, k3.

Row 2 (WS): K3, p to last 3 sts, k3.

Rows 3-6: Repeat last 2 rows twice more.

Switch to **Yarn C**.

Rows 7-12: Repeat **Rows 1-6**.

Continue in this way, switching yarns every 6 rows and repeating **Rows 7-12** with each colour, in the following sequence of colours: D, E, F, G, H, C, I, F, D, B, A, C, E, G, F, A, I, D, H, E, B, G, C, F, E, I, G, H, C, A, B, D, F, I, B, H, G, E, I, D, H, A.

Garter Stitch Edge

Switch to **Yarn A**.

Row 1 (RS): K2, (k1, m1L, k6, CDD, k6, m1R) to last 3 sts, k3.

Row 2 (WS): K.

Rows 3-4: Repeat last 2 rows once more.

Cast off.

Finishing

- Block blanket (see Finishing: Blocking) and lie flat to dry, shaping to measurements provided.

- Weave in all ends (see Tutorial 3: Weaving in ends on stocking stitch).

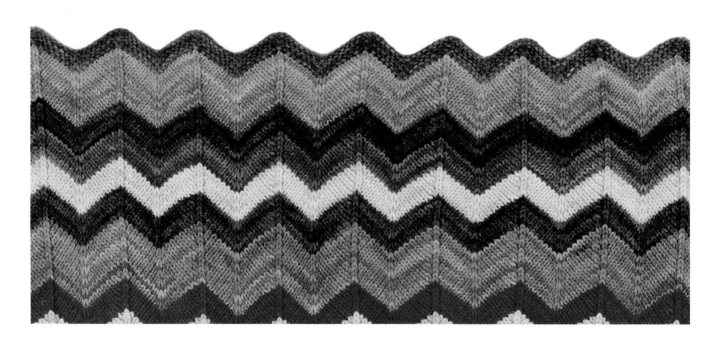

Tutorial 3: Weaving in ends on stocking stitch

When you knit in stripes, you will always have lots of ends to weave in from each change of colour. This can look a little messy at first, but once these ends are carefully woven in, your blanket will have neat edges.

The blanket has three garter stitches at the edges so follow the previous instructions for weaving in ends (see Tutorial 2: Weaving in ends on garter stitch) until you get to the stocking stitch section.

1. Ensure that the 'wrong side' of your work is facing. Thread your loose end onto a needle. Run the needle under the closest purl bump and pull yarn through.

2. Turn your needle and insert it under the purl bump adjacent to the original purl bump that you went under. Take your needle under the purl bump below that is slightly to the right. Pull yarn through.

3. Turn your needle and insert it under the purl bump adjacent to the purl bump that you just went under and under the purl bump from the row above that you previously came through.

4. Continue in this way, following the path of the knitted yarn on the fabric until you have woven in a few more sts, or until you feel your end is secure. Cut yarn.

Striped Socks

Who doesn't love stripy socks? Of course, there are endless varieties of self-striping and patterned sock yarns for knitters to choose from, or you have the freedom to create your own stripes by combining your favourite shades with contrasting colours for the cuffs, heels and toes. For these socks I've chosen a light and bright hand-dyed yarn and a dark solid-coloured yarn. The colours are contrasting enough to create bold stripes, but the speckles in the hand-dyed yarn soften the effect and add some fun!

You will need

Yarn

- **Yarn A:** Hedgehog Fibres Sock (90% merino wool, 10% nylon), 400m/437yds per 100g skein, in shade Fly; 1 skein

- **Yarn B:** Lang Jawoll (75% superwash wool, 18% nylon, 7% acrylic), 190m/207yds per 50g ball, in shade French Blue (235); 1 (1, 2) ball(s)

Needles and Accessories

- Five 2.5mm (US 1.5/UK 12 or UK 13) double-pointed needles (DPNS) or your preferred needles for working a small circumference in the round, or size needed to achieve correct tension

- Scrap yarn – a length of yarn about 50cm/20in that is a similar thickness to the sock yarn. Slippery yarn in a contrasting colour works best so that the yarn is easy to find and remove

- Stitch markers

Sizes

Small (Medium, Large)

- **To fit foot circumference:** 22 (24.5, 27)cm/ 8¾ (9¾, 10¾)in

- **Actual sock circumference:** 20 (22.5, 25)cm/ 8 (9, 10)in

- **Foot length:** Fully adjustable within the pattern

Skills

Casting on, knit, purl, decreasing, working in the round, grafting (Kitchener stitch)

Tension

36 sts and 50 rows to 10 x 10cm/4 x 4in over st st, using 2.5mm needles, after washing and blocking

Pattern

Make 2 the same, noting the placement of the heel for the right and left foot.

Cuff

Using **Yarn A**, cast on 64 (72, 80) sts and join in the round, taking care not to twist sts (see Advanced Knitting Techniques: Circular knitting).

Pm for start of round.

Round 1: *K2, p2; repeat from * to end of round.

Repeat **Round 1** until cuff measures 5cm/2in.

Leg

Join **Yarn B**.

Continue to work in stripes of 6 rounds, carrying the yarn not in use along the inside of the sock (see Tutorial 5: Carrying yarn up the round). To achieve a jogless stripe, use the jogless stripe method (see Tutorial 4: Jogless stripes).

**Rounds 1-6: K 6 rounds.

Switch to **Yarn A**.

Rounds 7-12: K 6 rounds.

Switch to **Yarn B**.**

Rounds 13-48: Repeat from ** to ** a further 3 times.

Rounds 49-54: K 6 rounds.

Switch to **Yarn A**.

Rounds 55-57: K 3 rounds.

Right Heel

Using a length of scrap yarn, k the next 32 (36, 40) sts.

Slip these sts back onto left-hand needle.

Using **Yarn A**, k these sts again and continue to end of round.

Left Heel

Knit 32 (36, 40) sts.

Using a length of scrap yarn, k the next 32 (36, 40) sts.

Slip these sts back to left-hand needle.

Using **Yarn A**, knit these sts again.

Foot

Continue in **Yarn A**.

Rounds 1-2: K 2 rounds.

Switch to **Yarn B**.

***Rounds 3-8: K 6 rounds.

Switch to **Yarn A**.

Rounds 9-14: K 6 rounds.

Switch to **Yarn B**.***

Repeat from *** to *** until foot measures no more than 13.5 (14.5, 15.5)cm/5¼ (5¾, 6)in long, measuring from heel placement round and ending after any 6-stripe section (noting that the toe will add 5.5 (6, 6) cm/2 (2½, 2½)in and the heel will add 7 (7.5, 8.5)cm/2¾ (3, 3¼)in).

Break off **Yarn A** and continue in **Yarn B** only.

Next round: K32 (36, 40), pm, k to end.

Toe

Round 1: K1, ssk, k to 3 sts before next marker, k2tog, k1, slm, k1, ssk, k to 3 sts before end of round, k2tog, k1 − 4 sts decreased.

Round 2: K all sts, slipping markers when you reach them.

Repeat the last 2 rounds a further 7 (9, 8) times − 32 (32, 44) sts remain.

Repeat **Round 1** only a further 3 (3, 5) times − 20 (20, 24) sts remain.

Next round: K to marker.

Cut yarn leaving a 30cm/12in tail.

Divide sts evenly over 2 needles and graft the toe closed using Kitchener stitch (see Advanced Knitting Techniques: Kitchener stitch).

Heel

Pick up the 32 (36, 40) sts from the round below the waste yarn, over 2 DPNS, by using the tip of the needle to lift the right leg of the stitch onto the DPN (see Advanced Knitting Techniques: Afterthought heel and thumb).

Rotate the sock and pick up the 32 (36, 40) sts on the opposite side of the waste yarn in the same manner, over 2 DPNS. Carefully remove the waste yarn, ensuring that all sts are secure on the needles.

Using **Yarn B**, begin working in the round as follows:

Round 1: Pick up and k 1 st in centre of the gap between the top and bottom of the heel, k32 (36, 40), pick up and k 2 sts in the gap between the top and bottom of the heel, k32 (36, 40), pick up and k 1 st, pm to mark end of round – 68 (76, 84) sts.

Round 2: K all sts.

Round 3: K34 (38, 42), pm, k to end.

Round 4: *K1, ssk, k to 3 sts before marker, k2tog, k1, slip marker; repeat from * once more – 64 (72, 80) sts.

Round 5: K all sts.

Repeat the last 2 rounds a further 10 (12, 14) times – 24 sts.

Cut yarn, leaving a 30cm/12in tail.

Divide sts evenly over 2 needles and graft the heel closed using Kitchener stitch (see Advanced Knitting Techniques: Kitchener stitch).

Finishing

- Block socks (see Finishing: Blocking).

- Weave in all ends.

Tutorial 4: Jogless stripes

When you knit in the round you are knitting in a continuous spiral, and so the end of one round is slightly higher than the beginning of the round. This means that when you change colours to knit stripes, the change of colour is clearly visible where the start and ends of the round meet. We call this the 'jog'. You can embrace the 'jog' or disguise the 'jog' quite effectively using this technique, which is worked at the beginning of each stripe.

1. Knit 1 full round in the new colour (image 1).

2. Before you start the next round, use the right-hand needle to lift the right-hand strand of the stitch that sits below the first stitch on the left-hand needle up and onto the tip of the left-hand needle (image 2).

3. Knit these 2 stitches together (image 3).

This will create an elongated stitch that disguises the jog and keeps your stripes looking neat (image 4).

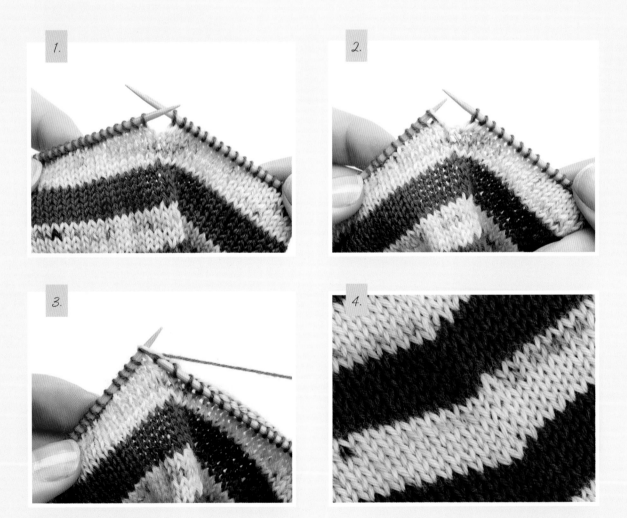

Tutorial 5: Carrying yarn up the round

This technique helps you to avoid breaking off the yarn after each stripe. This saves yarn and means that you won't have to sew in loose ends for every colour change. You will have both colours attached to the knitting at all times, so it's a good idea to keep your balls of yarn separate and tidy, to avoid tangles.

1. When you change to a new colour, take the ball of yarn you are knitting with (the new colour) and wrap it anti-clockwise all the way around the yarn that you are carrying up (the old colour) (image 1). Knit the first few stitches of the round and then ensure that the carried yarn is secured snugly, but not too tightly, or it might pucker your knitted fabric.

2. Continue knitting with the new colour for 2-4 rounds.

3. Wrap the carried yarn anti-clockwise again in the same way as **Step 1** (image 2).

It's important to ensure that you wrap the yarn in a counter-clockwise direction so that the carried yarn does not show through the knitting, and also to add some elasticity to the fabric (image 3).

Illusion Cushion

Illusion knitting is a fun way to show off with stripes. The designs are knitted in a simple striped sequence and, by simply alternating between knit and purl stitches along some rows, you can create raised 'bumps' on the right side of the fabric, sometimes called a 'garter ridge'. From the front your knitting will look like simple thin stripes, but when you view your knitting at a sideways angle, from the cast-on or cast-off edge, the garter ridges stand out and reveal the hidden pattern. For this cushion design I've chosen a dark grey and pale blue for a high contrast. I've used cool colours and subdued tones for a calm and minimalist look.

You will need

Yarn

Berroco Vintage (52% acrylic, 40% wool, 8% nylon), 198m/217yds per 100g skein, in the following shades:

- **Yarn A:** Gringham (5120); 1 skein
- **Yarn B:** Storm (5109); 1 skein

Needles and Accessories

- Pair of 4mm (US 6/UK 8) needles or size needed to achieve correct tension
- Four buttons, measuring 18mm (¾in)

Sizes

One size: 35 x 35cm/13¾ x 13¾in, to fit a 40cm/15¾in or 45cm/17¾in cushion insert

Skills

Casting on, knit, purl, reading a chart, casting off

Tension

17 sts and 33 rows to 10 x 10cm/4 x 4in over st st, using 4mm needles, after washing and blocking

Pattern

Front

To make the cushion front, either read from the written instructions or follow the charted instructions. Carry yarn not being used along the side of the work (see Tutorial 6: Carrying yarn up the side of the knitting).

Written Instructions

Using **Yarn A**, cast on 62 sts.

*Row 1 (RS): K.

Row 2 (WS): K1, (k10, p10) to last st, k1.

Switch to **Yarn B**.

Row 3: K.

Row 4: K1, (p10, k10) to last st, k1.

Switch to **Yarn A**.*

Rows 5-20: Repeat from * to * a further 4 times.

**Row 21: K.

Row 22: K1, (p10, k10) to last st, k1.

Switch to **Yarn B**.

Row 23: K.

Row 24: K1, (k10, p10) to last st, k1.

Switch to **Yarn A**.**

Rows 25-40: Repeat from ** to ** a further 4 times.

Rows 41-120: Repeat **Rows 1-40** twice more, then continue with buttonhole band (see Buttonhole Band).

Charted Instructions

Row 1 (RS): Reading chart from right to left, work **Row 1** of chart, working the pattern repeat area 3 times in total.

Row 2 (WS): Reading chart from left to right, work **Row 2** of chart, working the pattern repeat area 3 times in total.

Rows 3-40: Continue to work from chart as set, changing colours as indicated, until all 40 rows have been completed.

Rows 41-120: Repeat **Rows 1-40** twice more, then continue with buttonhole band (see Buttonhole Band).

Note

When finished, display your cushion sideways, with the button band running along the back vertically, in order to view the illusion pattern more easily.

Cushion Chart

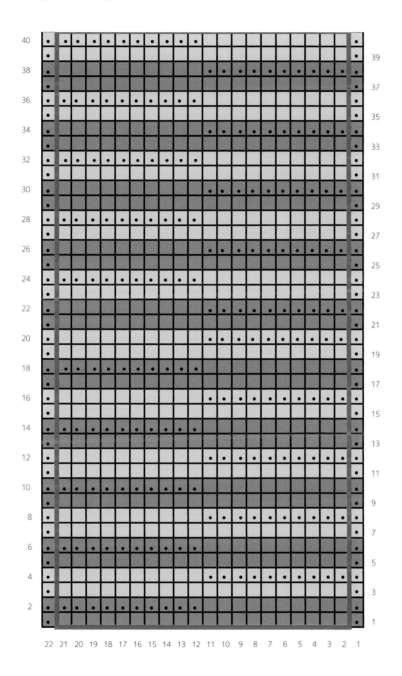

	Pattern repeat area
	Yarn A
	Yarn B
•	K on RS, K on WS
	K on RS, P on WS

Buttonhole Band

Switch to **Yarn A**.

Row 1: K.

Row 2: K1, (k2, p2) to last st, k1.

Row 3: K.

Row 4: K1, (p2, k2) to last st, k1.

Rows 5-12: Repeat **Rows 1-4** twice more.

Row 13: K.

Row 14: K1, (k2, p2) to last st, k1.

Row 15 (buttonhole row): K10, k2tog, yrn, (k11, k2tog, yrn) 3 times, k11.

Row 16: K1, (p2, k2) to last st, k1.

Rows 17-20: Repeat the last 4 rows once more.

Cast off.

Back

Using **Yarn A**, cast on 62 sts.

Rows 1-40: Work as given for Front.

Repeat **Rows 1-40** once more.

Repeat **Rows 1-20** once more.

Button Band

Switch to **Yarn A**.

Row 1: K.

Row 2: K1, (k2, p2) to last st, k1.

Row 3: K.

Row 4: K1, (p2, k2) to last st, k1.

Rows 5-20: Repeat **Rows 1-4** a further 4 times.

Cast off.

Finishing

- Block cushion to measurements provided (see Finishing: Blocking).

- Join the buttonhole band and the button band by placing the buttonhole band over the button band and seaming the sides with backstitch.

- Join the cushion sides along the other three sides using mattress stitch (see Finishing: Mattress stitch).

- Sew four buttons on the button band, using the buttonholes as a guide for placing them.

- Weave in all ends.

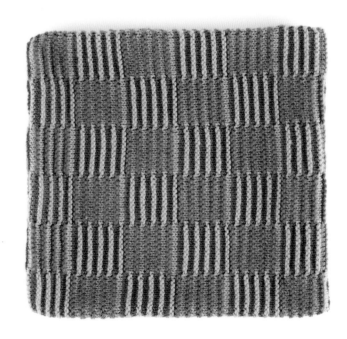

Tutorial 6: Carrying yarn up the side of the knitting

Illusion knitting is worked over a two-colour stripe pattern with two rows of knitting per stripe. You wouldn't want to break the yarn at every stripe, so it's better to carry the yarn up the side of the work. Over stripes that are two rows deep, this is extremely easy.

1. After knitting 2 rows with 1 colour, hold the colour that you have finished with at the back of your work (image 1).

2. Knit the next stitch with the new colour, ensuring that you have pulled the yarn snugly but not too tightly, or it might pucker the side of the fabric (image 2).

3. For stripes that are more than 2 rows deep you can still carry the yarn up the side of the work. Keep the sides neat and even by twisting the working yarn (the yarn you are using) around the carried yarn (the yarn you are not using) every couple of rows (image 3). Keep an eye on your tension as you do this.

Slipped Stitches

Brick Stitch Washcloths

Washcloths are ideal for trying new techniques. As well as being small, they're quite forgiving; they don't have to fit anything and any mistakes won't affect their usefulness! These washcloths use slipped stitches at the sides of the work to create a neat edge, as well as along the main textured pattern. I've chosen gentle, natural colours with enough contrast to emphasise the colourwork pattern. This is a great design for trying out any colour combinations that you can think of as you're only combining two colours, and the different areas of colours are quite distinct. Seeing as you won't be wearing them, you can go wild with colour choices and try out combinations that you wouldn't normally go for.

You will need

Yarn

Lily Sugar 'n Cream (100% cotton), 109m/119yds per 71g ball, in the following shades:

Lilac washcloth:

- **Yarn A:** Jute (0082); 1 ball
- **Yarn B:** Lilac (0093); 1 ball

Green washcloth:

- **Yarn A:** Jute (0082); 1 ball
- **Yarn B:** Sage Green (0084); 1 ball

Needles and Accessories

- Pair of 4.5mm (US 7/UK 7) needles or size needed to achieve correct tension

Size

One size: 24 x 24cm/9½ x 9½in

Skills

Casting on, knit, purl, slipped stitches, working in rows, reading a chart, casting off

Tension

18 sts and 36 rows to 10 x 10cm/4 x 4in over brick stitch pattern, using 4.5mm needles, after washing and blocking

Pattern

Using **Yarn A**, cast on 43 sts.

For **Rows 1-12**, either read from the written instructions or follow the charted instructions below. Read through the slipping stitches tutorial (see Tutorial: Slipping stitches) before starting your washcloth.

Written Instructions

Row 1 (RS): K to last 2 sts, sl2wyib.

Row 2 (WS): P to last 2 sts, sl2wyif.

Switch to **Yarn B**.

Row 3: K6, (sl1wyib, k5) to last 7 sts, sl1wyib, k4, sl2wyib.

Row 4: P2, k4, (sl1wyif, k5) to last 7 sts, sl1wyif, k4, sl2wyif.

Row 5: K2, p4, (sl1wyib, p5) to last 7 sts, sl1wyib, p4, sl2wyib.

Row 6: Repeat **Row 4**.

Switch to **Yarn A**.

Row 7: K to last 2 sts, sl2wyib.

Row 8: P to last 2 sts, sl2wyif.

Switch to **Yarn B**.

Row 9: K3, (sl1wyib, k5) to last 4 sts, sl1wyib, k1, sl2wyib.

Row 10: P2, k1, (sl1wyif, k5) to last 4 sts, sl1wyif, k1, sl2wyif.

Row 11: K2, p1, (sl1wyib, p5) to last 4 sts, sl1wyib, p1, sl2wyib.

Row 12: Repeat **Row 10**.

Repeat **Rows 1-12** a further 6 times.

Repeat **Rows 1-2**.

Cast off.

Washcloth Chart

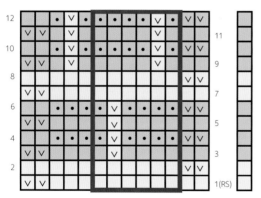

Column on the right shows the colour of yarn in use for the row

	Pattern repeat area		·	K on RS, K on WS
	Yarn A			K on RS, P on WS
	Yarn B		V	Sl1 with yarn on WS

Charted Instructions

Row 1 (RS): Reading chart from right to left, work first 2 sts of **Row 1** of the chart, work the pattern repeat area 6 times in total, then work the last 5 sts.

Row 2 (WS): Reading chart from left to right, work first 5 sts of **Row 2** of the chart, work the pattern repeat area 6 times in total, then work the last 2 sts.

Last 2 rows set position of chart pattern.

Rows 3-12: Continue to work from chart as set, until all 12 rows have been completed.

Repeat **Rows 1-12** a further 6 times.

Repeat **Rows 1-2**.

Cast off.

Finishing

- Block washcloth (see Finishing: Blocking).

- Weave in all ends.

Tutorial 7: Slipping stitches

Slipped stitches should always be slipped 'purlwise' unless directions state to slip a stitch 'knitwise'.

Another thing to consider is whether the working yarn should be held at the 'front' or 'back' of the knitting as you slip the stitch. This can get confusing as we also talk about a 'wrong side' or 'right side' of the knitting! I'll explain these differences here but don't worry about them too much because everything is clearly explained for each design.

Front and back

The 'front' of your knitting is the side that is facing you as you are working.

The 'back' of your knitting is the side that is not facing you as you are working.

What we refer to as the 'front' and 'back' of your knitting change as you turn your work.

Right side and wrong side rows

The 'right side' of your knitting is the side that is intended to be displayed.

The 'wrong side' of your knitting is the side that is not intended to be displayed.

The right and wrong side of your knitting will always be consistent and will be stated on the first two rows of the pattern instructions.

Slip 1 with yarn in back (sl1wyib)

Slip the next stitch purlwise with the working yarn held away from you at the back of the work as follows: with yarn at back of work, slip the next stitch purlwise (inserting the right-hand needle as if to purl the stitch (image 1) and slip it off the left-hand needle and onto the right-hand needle).

Slip 1 with yarn in front (sl1wyif)

Slip the next stitch purlwise with the working yarn held towards you at the front of the work as follows: bring the yarn between the needles to the front of the work. Slip the next stitch purlwise (inserting the right-hand needle as if to purl the stitch (image 2) and slip it off the left-hand needle and onto the right-hand needle). Take the yarn between the needles to the back of the work, ready to knit the next stitch.

Linen Stitch Bag

As with so many of the designs in this book, this project is deceptively simple to knit and yet the results look impressive. The striking pattern is worked across the entire fabric by slipping stitches alternately between knitted and purled stitches. Bright contrasting colours may look too busy, so I've toned down the look by choosing three colours that are close to each other on the colour wheel, two blues and a chartreuse yellow.

You will need

Yarn

BC Garn Semilla Grosso (100% organic wool), 80m/87yds per 50g ball, in the following shades:

- **Yarn A:** Gorgeous Turquoise (OA111); 2 balls
- **Yarn B:** Duck Egg (OA120); 1 ball
- **Yarn C:** Chartreuse (OA107); 1 ball

Needles and Accessories

- Pair of 5.5mm (US 9/UK 5) needles or size needed to achieve correct tension
- Pair of 6.5mm (US 10.5/UK 3) needles or a similar large size, for casting off only

Size

One size: 32 x 28cm/12½ x 11in

Skills

Casting on, knit, purl, slipped stitches, working in rows, reading a chart, casting off

Tension

18 sts and 35 rows to 10 x 10cm/4 x 4in over st st, using 5.5mm needles, after washing and blocking

Pattern

Front and Back

Make 2 the same.

Using **Yarn A**, cast on 55 sts.

For **Rows 1-6**, either read from the written instructions, or follow the charted instructions below. Read through the linen stitch tutorial (see Tutorial 8: Tricolour linen stitch) before starting your bag.

Written Instructions

Switch to **Yarn B**.

Row 1 (RS): K1, (sl1wyif, k1) to end.

Switch to **Yarn C**.

Row 2 (WS): K1, p1, (sl1wyib, p1) to last st, k1.

Switch to **Yarn A**.

Row 3: Repeat **Row 1**.

Switch to **Yarn B**.

Row 4: Repeat **Row 2**.

Switch to **Yarn C**.

Row 5: Repeat **Row 1**.

Switch to **Yarn A**.

Row 6: Repeat **Row 2**.

Charted Instructions

Row 1 (RS): Reading chart from right to left, work **Row 1** of the chart, working the pattern repeat area 26 times in total.

Row 2 (WS): Reading chart from left to right, work **Row 2** of the chart, working the pattern repeat area 26 times in total.

Rows 3-6: Continue to work from chart as set until all 6 rows have been completed.

For Written and Charted Instructions

Continue as follows:

Rows 7-102: Repeat **Rows 1-6** a further 16 times.

Break off **Yarns B and C** and continue in **Yarn A** only.

Row 103: K1, (sl1wyif, k1) to end.

Row 104: K1, p1, (sl1wyib, p1) to last st, k1.

Rows 105-114: Repeat the last 2 rows a further 5 times.

Using a larger needle size, cast off loosely in pattern as follows:

Casting off: K1, *sl1, lift lower stitch on right-hand needle over the top st (to cast off), k1, slip lower stitch on right-hand needle over top stitch (to cast off); repeat from * to end, break off yarn and pull yarn through the remaining stitch to fasten off.

Bag Handles

Make 2 the same.

Using **Yarn A**, cast on 7 sts.

Row 1 (RS): K1, (sl1wyif, k1) to end.

Row 2 (WS): K1, p1, (sl1wyib, p1) to last st, k1.

Repeat the last 2 rows until handles measure 58cm/23in.

Using a larger needle size, cast off loosely in pattern as given for casting off row for front and back panels.

Finishing

- Block bag (see Finishing: Blocking).

- Join the front and back panels along the bottom and sides with mattress stitch (see Finishing: Mattress stitch).

- Attach the handles by sewing them securely to the inside of the bag with an overlap of about 3cm/1¼in.

- Weave in all ends.

Bag Chart

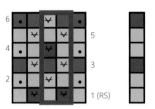

Column on the right shows the colour of yarn in use for the row

- ☐ Pattern repeat area
- ■ Yarn A
- ▨ Yarn B
- ▨ Yarn C
- ⊡ K on RS, K on WS
- ☐ K on RS, P on WS
- ⌣ Sl1 with yarn on RS

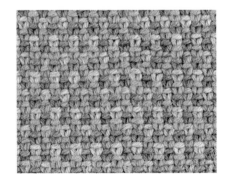

Linen stitch from right side

Linen stitch from wrong side

Tutorial 8: Tricolour linen stitch

Tricolour linen stitch is worked in the same way as regular linen stitch – the only difference is that the yarn colour is changed every row in a repeated sequence of three different colours.

When slipping stitches for this pattern it's helpful to remember that you always take the working yarn to the right side of the work before you slip the stitch and return it to the wrong side afterwards. This will form a horizontal 'bar' of yarn that is an essential part of the finished pattern. As the colour changes every row, you don't need to break the yarn after every stripe, just pick up the next colour that you need to knit with – and try not to get in a tangle!

Right-side rows

On right-side rows (where the right side of the work is facing you as you knit) you will alternate between knit 1 stitch and slip 1 stitch, with the yarn in front, as follows:

1. Knit 1 stitch.

2. Sl1wyif – slip 1 stitch purlwise with yarn in front. Bring the yarn between the needles to the front of the work. Slip the next stitch purlwise (inserting the right-hand needle as if to purl the stitch (image 1) and slip it off the left-hand needle and onto the right-hand needle). Take the yarn between the needles to the back of the work, ready to knit the next stitch (image 2).

Repeat **Steps 1 and 2** until the last stitch. Knit the last edge stitch.

Wrong-side rows

On wrong-side rows (where the wrong side of the work is facing you as you knit) you will alternate between purl 1 stitch and slip 1 stitch, with the yarn at the back as follows:

1. Knit 1 edge stitch.

2. Purl 1 stitch.

3. Sl1wyib – slip 1 stitch purlwise with yarn at the back. Take the yarn between the needles to the back of the work. Slip the next stitch purlwise (inserting the right-hand needle as if to purl the stitch (image 3) and slip it off the left-hand needle and onto the right-hand needle). Bring the yarn forward between the needles to the front of the work, ready to purl the next stitch (image 4).

Repeat **Steps 2 and 3** until the last stitch. Knit the last edge stitch.

Mosaic Mitts

These mitts are knitted in the round using the mosaic knitting technique. Stitches are knitted or slipped purlwise along each round to make up part of a larger-scale pattern. The effect is similar to stranded knitting. However, as only one colour is used for each round it is considered easier to work. These mitts feature a cross motif, limited to the wrists, adding interest to an otherwise minimal design. A strong colour contrast helps the slipped stitch pattern stand out. Whilst the main colour I've used is quite pale, it is still distinct alongside the much paler colour around the cross motif.

You will need

Yarn

Quince & Co. Tern (75% wool, 25% silk), 202m/221yds per 50g skein, in the following shades:

- **Yarn A:** Kelp; 1 skein
- **Yarn B:** Oyster; 1 skein

Needles and Accessories

- Set of five 2.75mm (US 2/UK 12) double-pointed needles (DPNS) or your preferred needles for working a small circumference in the round, or size needed to achieve correct tension

- Scrap yarn – a length of yarn about 50cm/20in that is a similar thickness to the yarn being used. Slippery yarn in a contrasting colour works best so that the yarn is easy to find and remove

- Stitch markers

Size

One size: to fit an average adult's hand

- **To fit hand circumference:** 18-20cm/7-8in

- **Actual mitt circumference:** 18.5cm/7¼in

- **Length:** 19cm/7½in

Skills

Casting on, knit, purl, reading a chart, knitting in the round, stranded colourwork, casting off, afterthought thumb method

Tension

26 sts and 40 rows to 10 x 10cm/4 x 4in over stranded st st, using 2.75mm needles, after washing and blocking

Pattern

Cuff

Using **Yarn A**, cast on 48 sts and join to work in the round, taking care not to twist sts (see Advanced Knitting Techniques: Circular knitting).

Pm for start of round.

Round 1: *K1, p1; repeat from * to end of round.

Rounds 2-3: Repeat last round twice more.

Round 4: K.

Mosaic Section

For **Rounds 1-26**, either read from the written instructions or follow the charted instructions below. Read through the tutorial for slipping stitches in mosaic knitting (see Tutorial 9: Slipping stitches in the round) before starting your mittens.

Written Instructions

Switch to **Yarn B**.

Round 1: *K2, (sl1, k1) 4 times, k2; repeat from * to end.

Round 2: Repeat **Round 1**.

Switch to **Yarn A**.

Round 3: *K1, sl1, k7, sl1, k2; repeat from * to end.

Round 4: Repeat **Round 3**.

Switch to **Yarn B**.

Round 5: *Sl1, k3, sl1, k1, sl1, k3, sl1, k1; repeat from * to end.

Round 6: Repeat **Round 5**.

Switch to **Yarn A**.

Round 7: *(K3, sl1) twice, k4; repeat from * to end.

Round 8: Repeat **Round 7**.

Switch to **Yarn B**.

Round 9: *(Sl1, k1) twice, k4, (sl1, k1) twice; repeat from * to end.

Round 10: Repeat **Round 9**.

Switch to **Yarn A**.

Round 11: *(K3, sl1) twice, k4; repeat from * to end.

Round 12: Repeat **Round 11**.

Switch to **Yarn B**.

Round 13: *Sl1, k3, (sl1, k1) twice, k2, sl1, k1; repeat from * to end.

Round 14: Repeat **Round 13**.

Switch to **Yarn A**.

Round 15: *K1, sl1, k7, sl1, k2; repeat from * to end.

Round 16: Repeat **Round 15**.

Switch to **Yarn B**.

Rounds 17-26: Repeat **Rounds 1-10**.

Charted Instructions

Joining in **Yarn B**, work from chart as follows:

Round 1: Reading chart from right to left, repeat **Row 1** of the chart 4 times.

Round 2: Repeat **Round 1**.

Last round sets the position of the mosaic colourwork pattern.

Rounds 3-26: Continue to work from chart as set until all 26 rounds have been completed.

Mitten Chart

Column on the right shows the colour of yarn in use for the round

Remember that each row of the chart represents two rounds of knitting

- ▨ Yarn A
- ☐ Yarn B
- ☐ Knit
- ☑ Sl1 with yarn on WS

Hand

Continue in **Yarn A** only.

Rounds 1-3: K.

Round 4: K23, pm, m1L, k2, m1R, pm, K23 – 50 sts.

Rounds 5-6: K.

Round 7: K to marker, slm, m1L, k to marker, m1R, slm, k to end – 52 sts.

Rounds 8-22: Repeat **Rounds 5-7** a further 5 times – 62 sts.

Round 23: K.

Round 24: K to marker, slip next 16 sts onto scrap yarn, cast on 2 sts using the knitted cast on method (see Getting Started: Knitted cast on), or your own preferred method, k to end – 48 sts.

Rounds 25-44: K 20 rounds.

Round 45: (K1, p1) to end.

Rounds 46-51: Repeat **Round 45** a further 6 times.

Cast off in pattern.

Thumb

Using **Yarn A**, pick up and knit 2 sts at the backwards loop cast on edge at thumb base, pick up and knit 16 sts from scrap yarn and join to work in the round, taking care not to twist sts (see Advanced Knitting Techniques: Circular knitting) – 18 sts.

Rounds 1-6: K 6 rounds.

Round 7: (K1, p1) to end.

Rounds 8-10: Repeat **Round 7** a further 3 times.

Cast off in pattern.

Finishing

- Block mittens (see Finishing: Blocking).

- Weave in all ends.

Tutorial 9: Slipping stitches in the round

As these mitts are knitted in the round, the right side of the work will always be facing you. This simplifies the process of slipping stitches as the yarn will always be held in the back, and it's easier to see your pattern emerge.

Every two rounds are worked the same. Remember that one row of your chart represents two rounds of knitting, and as you're working in the round, you always read the chart from right to left.

1. For the first two rounds you will be knitting with **Yarn B** and slipping **Yarn A** (image 1).

2. For the next two rounds you will be knitting with **Yarn A** and slipping **Yarn B** (image 2).

3. Continue alternating every two rounds between the yarn you slip and the yarn you knit, to continue the pattern.

Thorn Stitch Shawl

The elaborate-looking stitch pattern on this shawl is knitted using slipped stitches, increases and decreases. After a few repeats it becomes intuitive to knit and makes for a relaxing project. The shawl is finished with a couple of rows of garter stitch and a picot cast off. I've chosen two semi-solid hand-dyed yarns for this shawl with a very high contrast so that the pattern really stands out. I've kept my colour choice simple by using a light and a dark version of a pink-purple hue.

You will need

Yarn

Tosh Merino Light 4ply (100% merino wool), 384m/420yds per 100g skein, in the following shades:

- **Yarn A:** Scout; 1 skein
- **Yarn B:** Phantasm; 1 skein

Needles and Accessories

- Pair of 3.75mm (US 5/UK 9) needles or size needed to achieve correct tension

Size

One size

- **Wingspan:** 180cm/71in
- **Centre depth:** 56cm/22in

Skills

Casting on, knit, purl, slip stitches, increasing, decreasing, reading a chart, casting off

Tension

22 sts and 36 rows to 10 x 10cm/4 x 4in over thorn stitch pattern, using 3.75mm needles, after washing and blocking

Pattern

Using **Yarn A**, cast on 2 sts.

Garter Stitch Tab

Rows 1-6: Purl.

Turn and pick up and purl 3 sts along knitted edge.

Pick up and purl 2 sts at other end – 7 sts.

Shawl Set-up

Row 1 (RS): P2, YO, k1, m1R, pm, k1, pm, m1L, k1, YO, p2 – 11 sts.

Row 2 (WS): P2, YO, p to last 2 sts, YO, p2 – 13 sts.

Row 3: P2, YO, k4, m1R, k1, m1L, k4, YO, p2 – 17 sts.

Row 4: Repeat **Row 2** – 19 sts.

Main Shawl

For **Rows 1-8**, either read from the written instructions, or follow the charted instructions below. When working the slipped stitches, always slip the stitches with yarn on wrong side of work. This means that when you are working a knit (right side) row, you will slip the stitches with the yarn at the back (wyib) and when you work a purl (wrong side) row, you will slip the stitches with yarn in front (wyif). Read through Tutorial 10: Thorn stitch before starting your shawl. Slip markers when you reach them.

Note

Use stitch markers to mark each side of the central stitch. After placing markers, simply slip them as you come to them, always keeping them on each side of the central stitch.

Shawl Chart

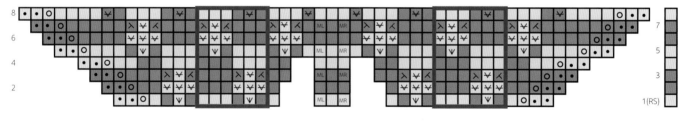

Column on the right shows the colour of yarn in use for the row

⬜ Yarn A	⬜ Knit on RS, purl on WS	ⱴ KYOK
🟦 Yarn B	• Purl	ⱴ Slip stitch purlwise
🟦 No stitch (move on to next instruction)	O Yarn over	⅄ Slip, slip, knit
⬜ Pattern repeat area		

ⱶ Knit 2 together
ML M1L
MR M1R

Written Instructions

Row 1: P2, YO, k1, (KYOK, k3) to 2 sts before first m, KYOK, k1, m1R, k1, m1L, k1, (KYOK, k3) to last 4 sts, KYOK, k1, YO, p2 – 31 sts.

Switch to **Yarn B**.

Row 2: P2, YO, p2, (sl3, p3) to 5 sts before first m, sl3, p5, (sl3, p3) to last 7 sts, sl3, p2, YO, p2 – 33 sts.

Row 3: P2, YO, k2, (k2tog, sl1, ssk, k1) to first m, m1R, k1, m1L, k1, (k2tog, sl1, ssk, k1) to last 3 sts, k1, YO, p2 – 29 sts.

Switch to **Yarn A**.

Row 4: P2, YO, p2, (sl1, p3) to last 5 sts, sl1, p2, YO, p2 – 31 sts.

Row 5: P2, YO, (k3, KYOK) to 1 st before first m, k1, m1R, k1, m1L, k1, (KYOK, k3) to last 2 sts, YO, p2 – 47 sts.

Switch to **Yarn B**.

Row 6: P2, YO, p4, (sl3, p3) to 5 sts before first m, sl3, p5, (sl3, p3) to last 3 sts, p1, YO, p2 – 49 sts.

Row 7: P2, YO, k4, (K2tog, sl1, ssk, k1) to first m, m1R, k1, m1L, (k1, k2tog, sl1, ssk) to last 6 sts, k4, YO, p2 – 41 sts.

Switch to **Yarn A**.

Row 8: P2, YO, p4, (sl1, p3) to last 3 sts, p1, YO, p2 – 43 sts.

Charted Instructions

For an explanation of reading more complex charts, see Reading Charts.

Row 1 (RS): Reading chart from right to left, work **Row 1** of chart – 31 sts

Row 2 (WS): Reading the chart from left to right, work **Row 2** of chart – 33 sts

Last 2 rows set chart pattern.

Rows 3-8: Continue to work from chart as set until all 8 rows have been completed – 43 sts.

For Written and Charted Instructions

Repeat **Rows 1-8** a further 17 times – 451 sts.

Repeat **Rows 1-3** once more – 561 sts.

Border

Continue in **Yarn B** only.

Row 1: P.

Row 2: P2, k to first m, m1R, k1, m1L, k to last 2 sts, p2 – 563 sts.

Row 3: K.

Rows 4-5: Repeat **Rows 2-3** once more – 565 sts.

Work a picot cast off as follows:

*Cast on 2 sts, cast off 4 sts, slip last st to left-hand needle; repeat from * to last st, break off yarn and pull through remaining st to fasten off.

Finishing

- Block shawl (see Finishing: Blocking). If you would like to enhance the picot cast off, pin each picot out when blocking.

- Weave in all ends.

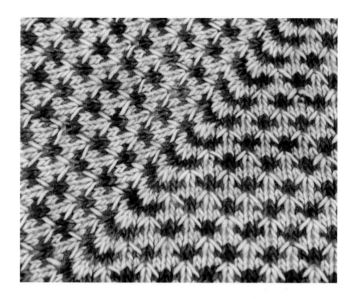

Tutorial 10: Thorn stitch

It's important to remember that when slipping stitches we slip them 'purlwise' as if we were going to purl the stitch. This is because slipping the stitches 'knitwise' would twist the stitch. Refer to the slipping stitches tutorial (see Tutorial 7: Slipping stitches) for more information on 'front' and 'back' of your knitting and for an explanation of 'right side' and 'wrong side'.

The thorn stitch pattern is worked with an eight row repeat over a multiple of 4 stitches, plus 1 stitch. To knit a swatch for this fabric you need to cast on a number of stitches that is a multiple of 4 plus an extra stitch (33 stitches should be enough to test the tension and practise the pattern). For your swatch, cast on using **Yarn A**.

To work the instructions 'KYOK', or K1, YO, K1 all into the next stitch, you need to knit into the stitch without sliding it off of the needle, work a yarn over around the right-hand needle, and then knit into the same stitch again, this time sliding it off of the needle. This is a double increase and will result in two extra stitches being made.

Row 1 (RS): Using **Yarn A**, k2, (KYOK (image 1), k3) to last 3 sts, KYOK, k2.

Row 2: Using **Yarn B**, p2, (sl3wyif (image 2), p3) to last 5 sts, sl3wyif, p2.

Row 3: Using **Yarn B**, k1, (k2tog, sl1wyib (image 3), ssk, k1) to end.

Row 4: Using **Yarn A**, p4, (sl1wyif (image 4), p3) to last st, p1.

Row 5: Using **Yarn A**, k4, (KYOK, k3) to last st, k1.

Row 6: Using **Yarn B**, p4, (sl3 wyif, p3) to last st, k1.

Row 7: Using **Yarn B**, k3, (k2tog, sl1wyib, ssk, k1) to last 2 sts, k2.

Row 8: Using **Yarn A**, p2, (sl1wyif (image 4), p3) to last 3 sts, sl1wyif, p2.

1.

2.

3.

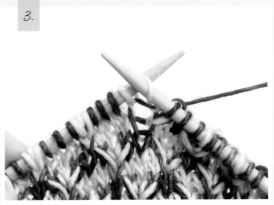

4.

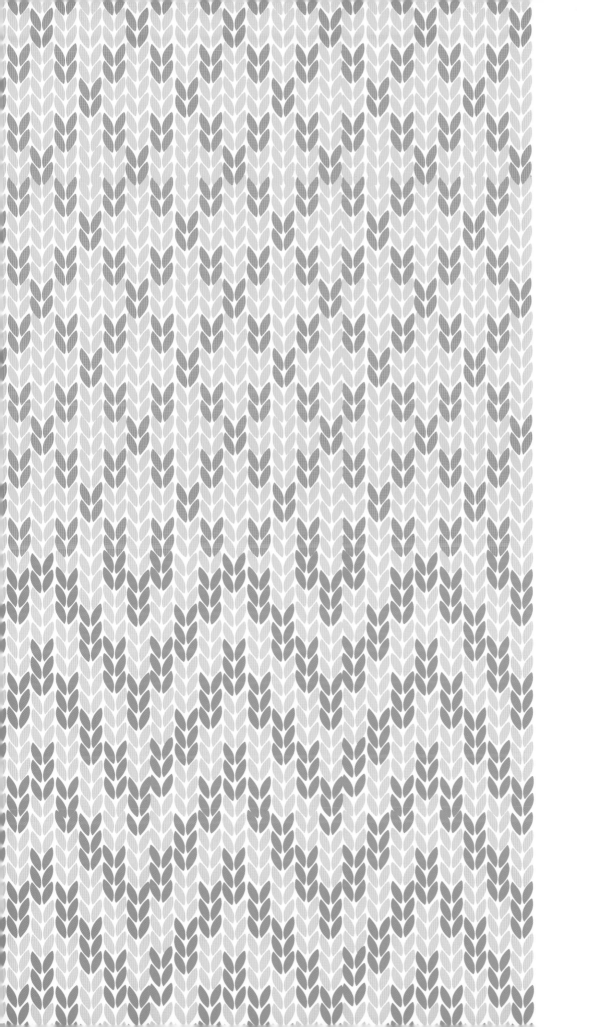

Stranded Colourwork

Monochrome Mitts

These mitts are an ideal introduction to stranded knitting, sometimes referred to as Fair Isle, a technique where the knitter uses two strands of yarn at a time to create the design. For this design I've used three colours – two greys and a pop of mustard on the cuffs and thumb. The high contrast between the two greys means that the colourwork pattern stands out boldly. I've chosen a woolly yarn that is ideal for colourwork. The fibres blend the stitches together neatly and the fuzzy 'stickiness' of the wool can help ensure that the floats aren't pulled too tightly along the back of the work.

You will need

Yarn

Baa Ram Ewe Pip Colourwork (100% wool), 116m/126yds per 25g ball, in the following shades:

- **Yarn A:** Brass Band; 1 ball
- **Yarn B:** Coal; 1 ball
- **Yarn C:** Crucible; 1 ball

Needles and Accessories

- Set of five 2.5mm (US 1.5/UK 13) DPNS or your preferred needles for working small circumferences in the round, or size needed to achieve correct tension
- Set of five 2.75mm (US 2/UK 12) DPNS, or size needed to achieve correct tension
- Scrap yarn – a length of yarn about 25cm/10in that is a similar thickness to the main yarn. Slippery yarns and a contrasting colour works best so that the yarn is easy to find and remove.
- Stitch markers

Sizes

Small (Medium, Large)

- **To fit hand circumference:** 17.5 (19, 20.5cm/ 6¾ (7½, 8)in
- **Actual mitt circumference:** 20 (21.5, 23)cm/ 7¾ (8½, 9)in
- **Length:** 19cm/7½in

Skills

Casting on, knit, purl, reading a chart, knitting in the round, stranded colourwork, afterthought thumb method, casting off

Tension

28 sts and 30 rows to 10 x 10cm/4 x 4in over stranded st st, using 2.75mm needles, after washing and blocking

Pattern

Read through Tutorials 11-14 on joining a new colour, yarn management, yarn dominance and keeping an even tension, before starting your mittens.

Finger Edge

Using 2.5mm DPNS and **Yarn A**, cast on 56 (60, 64) sts and join in the round, taking care not to twist sts (see Advanced Knitting Techniques: Circular knitting).

Pm for start of round.

Round 1: (K1, p1) to end of round.

Rounds 2-6: Repeat **Round 1** a further 5 times.

Hand

Switch to 2.75mm DPNS. Joining in **Yarn B** and **Yarn C**, work from chart as follows:

Round 1: Reading chart from right to left, work **Row 1** of the chart 14 (15, 16) times.

Last round set position of the stranded colourwork pattern.

Rounds 2-8: Continue to work from chart as set until all 8 rounds have been completed.

Rounds 9-16: Repeat **Rounds 1-8** once more.

Rounds 17-20: Repeat **Rounds 1-4** once more.

Thumb Placement – Left Hand

Using scrap yarn, knit the next 8 (9, 10) sts. Slip these sts back to left-hand needle.

Using **Yarn B** and **Yarn C** and following **Row 5** of the chart, knit these sts again and continue to end of round.

Thumb Placement – Right Hand

Following **Round 5** of the chart, knit to last 8 (9, 10) sts. Using scrap yarn, knit the next 8 (9, 10) sts. Slip these sts back to left-hand needle. Using **Yarn B** and **Yarn C** and continuing to follow **Row 5** of the chart, knit these sts again.

Hand

Rounds 1-3: Work **Rows 6-8** of the colourwork chart.

Rounds 4-27: Work **Rows 1-8** of the colourwork chart three times more.

Wrist Edge

Switch to 2.5mm DPNS. Join **Yarn A** and continue in **Yarn A** only.

Round 1: K.

Round 2: (K1, P1) to end of round.

Rounds 3-9: Repeat **Round 2** a further 7 times.

Cast off in pattern.

Thumb

Using 2.5mm DPNS and **Yarn A**, pick up 9 sts from above and 9 sts from below waste yarn, removing the waste yarn as you go – 18 sts.

Divide sts over 3 or 4 DPNS and use spare DPN to start knitting. Note that these stitches can look slightly messy when you first pick them up (see photo, showing sts on two DPNS). Don't worry, they will look fine once you have knitted over them.

Round 1: K9, pick up and k 1 st at the edge of the thumb opening, k across remaining sts, pick up and k 1 st at opposite corner of thumb opening, join to work in the round – 20 sts.

Round 2: (K1, p1) to end of round.

Repeat **Round 2** a further 4 times.

Cast off loosely in rib.

Finishing

- Block mittens (see Finishing: Blocking).

- Weave in all ends.

Mitts Chart

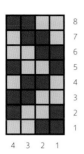

8
7
6
5
4
3
2
1

4 3 2 1

■ Yarn B

■ Yarn C

□ Knit

Tutorial 11: Joining a new colour

When you work a stranded colourwork pattern the instructions will often say to 'join Yarn B' and this can seem confusing, especially if, like me, you're prone to overthinking things! Joining a new colour is exactly the same as changing (or switching) colour for knitting stripes, but we use the word 'join' instead of 'change' because we will now be using two colours throughout the round.

To join a new colour simply start knitting with the new colour when indicated in your pattern, whether it's at the start of the round or elsewhere along the round (image 1).

1.

Tutorial 12: Yarn management

Stranded knitting requires the knitter to use two yarns for each colourwork round. While one yarn is being knitted with, the other yarn will be carried along the wrong side of the knitting, and these yarns will be switched throughout the round to form the colourwork pattern. Stranded knitting can be worked using different methods. For some of these methods, yarn is held by fingers and picked at by needles; with other methods, needles are held still and fingers move the yarn.

Managing both yarns while working a stranded colourwork round is something that can take some practise and experimentation. How you feel comfortable managing your yarn for colourwork may depend on your usual knitting technique. Personally, I knit in the English throwing style and I sometimes hold both yarns in my right hand, or sometimes I just pick up each yarn as I want to knit with it. I don't think that there is a wrong way to manage your yarns, as long as you are enjoying your knitting and you are pleased with the results. However, some knitters like to try these techniques to find which is most comfortable for them. Holding one colour in each hand is popular for knitters of stranded colourwork.

Holding both strands in your right hand

Holding one colour in each hand

Holding both yarns in your left hand

Holding both yarns in one hand over different fingers

Tutorial 13: Yarn dominance

However you choose to hold your yarns, you should try to keep the positions of the yarn untwisted to avoid tangles and to keep consistency in your yarn dominance. Yarn dominance refers to which colour yarn is most dominant in your knitted fabric. This occurs because the yarn strands, or floats, that are carried along the back of your work, lie in a different position for each colour depending on whether you are holding the yarn above or below the other. The yarn that is carried below the other is the dominant colour while the stitches made with the yarn from above will recede very slightly.

The colour that goes over will recede slightly (image 1).

The colour that comes from under will look dominant (image 2).

Some stranded colourwork patterns have a defined pattern and a background. In these cases it might be nice to experiment with yarn dominance. Alternatively you can just hold your yarns in a consistent way and not think about yarn dominance at all.

Tutorial 14: Keeping an even tension

A great tip for keeping your tension nice and even when stranding yarn is to work with the wrong side of your knitting on the outside. This prevents tight strands which can have a surprisingly dramatic affect on the tension, and therefore the finished measurements, of your project.

Start by casting on and knitting as usual. When you come to the stranded section simply turn your knitting inside out. You will be working with your stitches at the back of your work instead of the front. The right side of your knitting will still be visible in the inside of the tube.

I find this technique very effective. I always use it when I am knitting a project that alternates between stranded and plain sections of knitting to keep the tension even throughout.

Graphic Hat

This stranded hat is bright, bold, busy and just the kind of project I enjoy. The stranded colourwork covers all of the hat, including the crown shaping, but it doesn't require any particular skills. Just work the decreases in the same place along the round, so that the decrease lines become a feature of the design. I used five different colours for this hat, but you could use fewer if you prefer. I picked a mid-tone neutral colour for the ribbed brim. Over the stranded section, I've used two bright colours for the line detail and two very pale colours for the background.

You will need

Yarn

Jamieson's Shetland Spindrift 4ply (100% wool), 105m/115yds per 25g ball, in the following shades:

- **Yarn A:** Steel (320); 1 ball
- **Yarn B:** Jade (787); 1 ball
- **Yarn C:** Apricot (435); 1 ball
- **Yarn D:** Buttermilk (179); 1 ball
- **Yarn E:** Spice (526); 1 ball

Needles and Accessories

- Set of five 3.5mm (US 4/UK 9 or 10) DPNS or circular needles 40cm/15¾in long, or your preferred needles for knitting small circumferences in the round, or the size needed to achieve correct tension
- Stitch markers

Sizes

One size: to fit an average adult's head size

- **To fit head circumference:** 56-60cm/22-23½in
- **Actual hat circumference:** 50cm/19½in

Skills

Casting on, knit, purl, decreasing, working in the round, reading a chart, stranded colourwork, casting off

Tension

24 sts and 24 rows to 10 x 10cm/4 x 4in over st st, using 3.5mm needles, after washing and blocking

Pattern

Read through the tutorial on shaping with colourwork (see Tutorial 15: Shaping with colourwork) before starting your hat.

Brim

Using **Yarn A**, cast on 120 sts and join in the round, taking care not to twist sts (see Advanced Knitting Techniques: Circular knitting).

Pm for start of round.

Round 1: (K2, p2) to end of round.

Rounds 2-11: Repeat **Round 1** a further 10 times.

Main Body

Join **Yarn B** and **Yarn C**.

Round 1: Reading chart A from right to left, repeat the 8 sts of **Row 1** of the chart, 15 times.

Last round sets position of the stranded colourwork pattern.

Rounds 2-29: Joining **Yarn D** and **Yarn E** as required, continue to work from chart A as set, until all 29 rounds have been completed.

Crown

Continue in **Yarn D** and **Yarn E** only.

Round 1: Reading chart B from right to left, repeat the 24 sts of **Row 1** of the chart, 5 times.

Last round sets the position of the stranded colourwork pattern.

Rounds 2-23: Continue to work from chart B as set until all 23 rounds have been completed, working the central double decrease as set, to decrease 10 sts on the decrease rounds — 10 sts.

Break yarn and pull through remaining sts.

Finishing

- Block hat (see Finishing: Blocking) and lie flat to dry, shaping to measurements provided.

- Weave in ends.

Hat Chart A

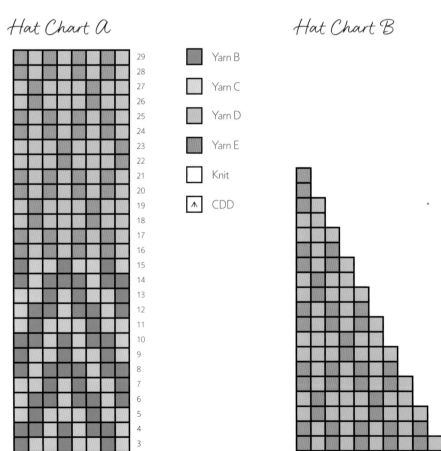

▨	Yarn B
░	Yarn C
▒	Yarn D
▓	Yarn E
☐	Knit
⋀	CDD

Hat Chart B

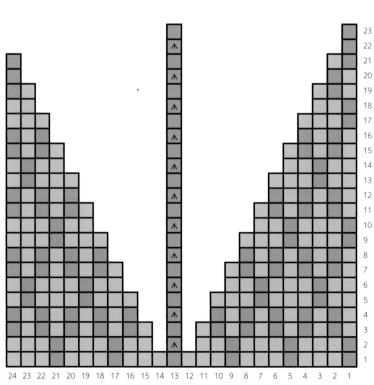

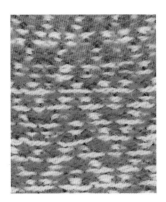

Tutorial 15: Shaping with colourwork

This hat design has a stranded colourwork pattern all the way over it and covering the crown. This means that you will be working deceases within the colourwork knitting. It's possible to work any increases or decreases within stranded knitting but it will affect the colourwork pattern and some methods may be more noticeably disruptive than others.

A centred double decrease (CDD) is a good choice for a visible yet neat decrease in colourwork knitting.

This centred double decrease is worked in the same way as when you are knitting with just one colour. It works effectively in stranded knitting by allowing a single colour to run up the decreased section in a straight line.

1. Work the pattern chart up to the CDD instructions.

2. Slip the next 2 stitches to right-hand needle, as if to knit 2 stitches together (image 1).

3. Using the colour indicated on the chart, knit next stitch (image 2).

4. Pass the 2 slipped stitches over the stitch just knitted (image 3).

The new stitch made will be in the correct colour and the stitch below will look neat and even in the colour used below.

Continue to work from chart, knitting the next stitch in the colour indicated on the chart.

1.

2.

3.

Chunky Ombre Hat

This bold, ombre hat is a quick and fun knit. Using bulky yarn for stranded colourwork makes the fabric extra thick and cosy. The colourwork pattern is worked around the sides of the hat while the shaping of the crown is worked in one colour only. As with most stranded projects, a high contrast between the colours helps to enhance the pattern. I've used pale neutrals alongside dark and rich jewel-tone colours. As the pattern itself is so bold, I've tried to use colour combinations that are subtle and easy to wear.

You will need

Yarn

Cascade 128 Superwash (100% merino wool), 117m/127yds per 100g skein, in the following shades:

Sample 1
* **Yarn A:** Dark Plum (1965); 1 skein
* **Yarn B:** Feather Grey (875); 1 skein

Sample 2
* **Yarn A:** Aporto (856); 1 skein
* **Yarn B:** Silver (1946); 1 skein

Sample 3
* **Yarn A:** Silver (1946); 1 skein
* **Yarn B:** Aporto (856); 1 skein

Needles and Accessories

* Pair of 5mm (US 8/UK 6) DPNS or your preferred needles for working small circumferences in the round, or size needed to achieve correct tension

Sizes

Child (Adult, Large Adult)

* **To fit head circumference:** 49 (56, 61)cm/ 19½ (22, 24)in

* **Actual hat circumference:** 48 (53, 58)cm/ 19 (21, 23)in

Skills

Casting on, knit, purl, decreasing, working in the round, reading a chart

Tension

15 sts and 18 rows to 10 x 10cm/4 x 4in over stranded colourwork, using 5mm needles, after washing and blocking

Pattern

Read through the tutorial on trapping floats (see Tutorial 16: Trapping floats) before starting your hat. The chart shows the colours for Sample 1.

Brim

Using **Yarn A**, cast on 72 (80, 88) sts and join in the round, taking care not to twist sts (see Advanced Knitting Techniques: Circular knitting).

Pm for start of round.

Round 1: (K1, p1) to end of round.

Repeat **Round 1** a further 2 (3, 4) times.

Main Body

Join **Yarn B**.

Round 1: Reading chart from right to left, repeat the sts of **Row 1** of the chart, 9 (10, 11) times.

Last round sets position of the stranded colourwork pattern.

Rounds 2-19: Continue to work from chart as set until all 18 rounds have been completed.

Continue with **Yarn B** only.

Round 20: K.

Repeat last round a further 1 (3, 4) times.

Crown

Round 1: (K6, k2tog) to end of round – 63 (70, 77) sts.

Round 2: K.

Round 3: (K5, k2tog) to end of round – 54 (60, 66) sts.

Round 4: K.

Round 5: (K4, k2tog) to end of round – 45 (50, 55) sts.

Round 6: K.

Round 7: (K3, k2tog) to end of round – 36 (40, 44) sts.

Round 8: K.

Round 9: (K2, k2tog) to end of round – 27 (30, 33) sts.

Round 10: K.

Round 11: (K1, k2tog) to end of round – 18 (20, 22) sts.

Round 12: K.

Round 13: K2tog to end of round – 9 (10, 11) sts.

Break off yarn and pull through remaining sts.

Finishing

- Block hat (see Finishing: Blocking) and lie flat to dry, shaping to measurements provided.

- Weave in all ends.

- Using **Yarn A**, make a pompom and attach it to the centre of the crown (see Finishing: Making a pompom).

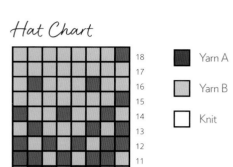

Hat Chart

Legend:
- Yarn A
- Yarn B
- Knit

Tutorial 16: Trapping floats

'Float' is another term for the strand of yarn that runs along the back of the stranded fabric. Most stranded colourwork patterns alternate between yarn colours every few stitches, keeping the floats quite short. When five or more stitches are worked between colour changes, the floats become quite long. In these cases, you may want to 'trap' the floats midway to keep them neat and secured to the fabric.

Following the steps below will help you achieve a smooth surface pattern with even stitches. The images show the colours for Sample 3. For this hat, floats were trapped on **Row 1** and **Row 18** of the chart after knitting three stitches in the main colour for the round. Note that the yarn to be floated needs to come underneath the working yarn (image 1).

1. When ready to trap yarn, insert the needle into the stitch to be knitted, but do not wrap your working yarn around the needle yet (image 2).

2. Slide the right-hand needle underneath the strand to be trapped/floated (the yarn will sit on top of the needle) (image 3).

3. Wrap the working yarn around the right-hand needle in the usual manner to knit the stitch (image 4).

4. Pull the needle back through the stitch as normal, trapping the yarn not in use (image 5).

5. Knit the next stitch, keeping the yarns in position. Continue working from the pattern, repeating these steps as required to trap long floats.

Steeked Mug Cosy

Most knitters prefer to work stranded colourwork in the round, but there are times when you would like your finished fabric to be used as a flat piece of knitting. That's where steeking can help! It may seem daunting cutting into your knitting so this mug cosy is an ideal practice project. It's such a quick little knit that it's easy to knit another if anything goes wrong (which it won't!). The gentle scallop pattern would suit most colour combinations. I've used a fuzzy, tweedy yarn for a softer look and a big natural shell button is the finishing touch.

You will need

Yarn

Rowan Felted Tweed DK (50% merino wool, 25% alpaca, 25% viscose), 175m/191yds per 50g ball, in the following shades:

- **Yarn A:** Watery (152); 1 ball
- **Yarn B:** Bilberry (151); 1 ball
- **Yarn C:** Avocado (161); 1 ball

Needles and Accessories

- Set of five 3.25mm (US 3/UK 10) DPNS or your preferred needles for working small circumferences in the round, or size needed to achieve correct tension
- A length of scrap yarn about 120cm/47in that is a similar thickness to the main yarn (strong yarns such as a sock yarn work best)
- One button
- A 3.25mm (US E/4) crochet hook

Size

One size: to fit average to large mug

- **Width:** 26cm/10¼in
- **Height:** 7cm/2¾in

Skills

Casting on, knit, purl, reading a chart, knitting in the round, stranded colourwork, crochet chain stitch, casting off

Tension

28 sts and 28 rows to 10 x 10cm/4 x 4in over stranded st st, using 3.25mm needles, after washing and blocking

Pattern

Using **Yarn A**, cast on 62 sts and join in the round, taking care not to twist sts (see Advanced Knitting Techniques: Circular knitting).

Round 1: (K1, p1) to last 6 sts, k6.

Round 2: Repeat **Round 1**.

Round 3: Reading chart from right to left, work the pattern repeat area of **Row 1** of the chart, 7 times, then work the last 6 sts.

Rounds 4-17: Continue to work from chart as set until all 14 rounds have been completed.

Continue in **Yarn A** only.

Round 18: K.

Round 19: Repeat **Round 1**.

Cast off in pattern.

Reinforce and cut the steek through the central steek st, marked on the colourwork chart as column 12 (see Tutorial 17: Steeking).

Edges

Work both edges the same.

Pick up and k 17 sts evenly between the steek sts and the colourwork knitting, marked on the chart as the edge between columns 9 and 10 for one edge and columns 14 and 1 for the other edge. Continue in rib:

Row 1: (K1, p1) to end.

Row 2: (P1, k1) to end.

Cast off in rib.

Button Loop

Using crochet hook, make a chain that is 6cm/2½in long.

Alternatively, knit an i-cord or use your preferred technique to make a button loop.

Knitting the Mug Cosy Flat

If preferred, to avoid steeking, you can also knit the mug cosy flat with a pair of straight 3.25mm needles as follows, referring to Tutorial 18: Knitting colourwork flat:

Using **Yarn A**, cast on 65 sts onto one 3.25mm straight needle.

Row 1: (K1, p1) to end, turn.

Row 2: Repeat **Row 1**.

Row 3: Reading chart from right to left for odd numbered rows, work the pattern repeat area of **Row 1** of the chart, 8 times then work column 9.

Row 4: Reading chart from left to right for even numbered rows, and ignoring columns 10-14, work column 9 then work the pattern repeat area of **Row 2** of the chart, 8 times.

Rows 5-16: Continue to work from chart as set until all 14 rounds have been completed.

Row 17: (K1, p1) to end, turn.

Row 18: Repeat **Row 17**.

Cast off in rib, then work button loop as given for steeked mug cosy.

Mug Cosy Chart

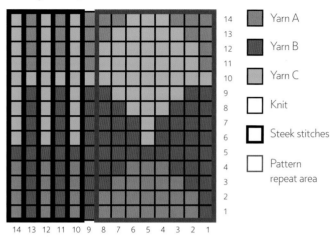

▦	Yarn A
▦	Yarn B
▦	Yarn C
☐	Knit
☐	Steek stitches
☐	Pattern repeat area

Finishing

- Block mug cosy (see Finishing: Blocking) and lie flat to dry, shaping to measurements provided.

- Weave in ends.

- Sew button loop on the ribbing of one edge and the button at the same height on the other edge.

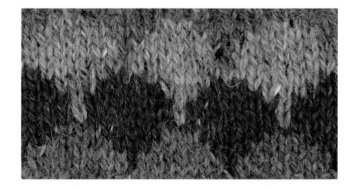

Tutorial 17: Steeking

Steeking is a stranded colourwork technique used to make knitted fabric that has been worked in the round open up to be used flat. Steeks are the extra stitches that are knitted in the place that is going to be cut open.

Steek stitches are usually worked over colourwork in vertical stripes to keep the fabric firmer and to carry both yarns across the steek section securely. After the knitting is completed the steeks are secured and cut open, which is not nearly as scary as it may sound!

Reinforcing the steek

First, reinforce the edges of the steek using the strong scrap yarn and a crochet hook. It's also possible to sew a reinforcement by hand or using a sewing machine. Then secure both edges of the central steek stitches as we are going to cut right along the middle of this central line of stitches.

1. Find your steek stitches and note the central st (image 1).

2. Using your length of strong scrap yarn, make a slip knot onto your crochet hook (image 2).

3. Insert your crochet hook through the stitch next to the central steek stitch (image 3).

4. Pull a loop of scrap yarn through the stitch on the knitting (2 loops on hook) (image 4). Then pull that loop of scrap yarn (the top loop) through the bottom loop, leaving just one loop on the crochet hook.

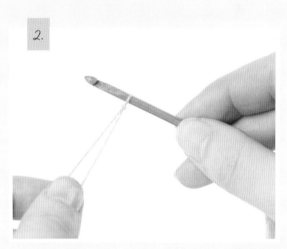

5. Insert the crochet hook through half of the stitch next to the central steek stitch and and half of the central steek stitch (image 5).

6. Pull a loop of scrap yarn through the stitches (image 6). Then pull that loop of scrap yarn through the other, as before, leaving one loop on the crochet hook.

7. Continue working **Steps 5-6** all the way along one edge of the central steek stitch (image 7). Then secure the end by working into the centre of the stitch next to the central steek stitch and fasten off the end.

8. Turn your knitting to work in the opposite direction and repeat all of the steps above, along the other side of the central steeked stitch (image 8).

Cutting the steek

Using a pair of small sharp scissors, cut along the ladder of strands between the reinforced edges (image 9).

Finishing the steek

1. Using Yarn A, pick up stitches along the edge of the steek between the steek stitches and the main pattern stitches (image 1).

2. Knit the edges as directed in the instructions (image 2).

3. To keep the edge neat and secure sew down the line of crochet (image 3).

Tutorial 18: Knitting colourwork flat

While some knitters prefer to avoid working stranded colourwork flat, others don't mind it.

Simply turn your work and purl your stitches, keeping the floats on the wrong side of the work. Ensure that you are following your colourwork chart in the right direction and that you remain consistent in which yarn is being worked above or below the other (see Tutorial 13: Yarn dominance).

Intarsia

Tassel Bunting

This bunting would make a great stash buster project as the flags can be made with small amounts of any DK yarn. The intarsia technique is used to give the bunting a colourful contrast border and a long tassel adds a cheerful, jubilant feel. I've chosen a range of colours; bright, subdued, light, and dark, from all around the colour wheel and I've mixed and matched the colours to make a vibrant string of party bunting. Alternatively you can restrict your colour palette and give your bunting a more tranquil look.

You will need

Yarn

Coop Knits Socks Yeah! DK (75% merino wool, 25% nylon), 211m/231yds per 50g skein, in the following shades:

- **Yarn A:** Demeter (209); 1 skein
- **Yarn B:** Fleet (212); 1 skein
- **Yarn C:** Morpheus (206); 1 skein
- **Yarn D:** Dionysus (205); 1 skein
- **Yarn E:** Pigeon (214); 1 skein
- **Yarn F:** Sphene (215); 1 skein
- **Yarn G:** Astra Planeti (203); 1 skein

Needles and Accessories

- Pair of 3.75mm (US 5/UK 9) needles or size needed to achieve correct tension
- A length of ribbon or yarn to thread the flags onto

Size

One size: Each flag is 15cm/6in wide and 13cm/6¾ in deep, without tassel

Skills

Casting on, knit, purl, decreasing, casting off

Tension

23 sts and 32 rows to 10 x 10cm/4 x 4in over st st, using 3.75mm needles, after washing and blocking

Pattern

For each flag, choose 2 colours to represent **Yarn A** and **Yarn B**. Then switch the **Yarn A** and **Yarn B** colours to make more flags. Read through the intarsia tutorial (see Tutorial 19: Intarsia) before starting your bunting.

Using **Yarn A**, cast on 35 sts.

Row 1 (RS): K.

Row 2 (WS): K.

Row 3: K1, (k2tog, YO) to last 2 sts, k2.

Rows 4-7: K.

Join **Yarn B**.

Row 8: K3 in **Yarn A**, k to last 3 sts in **Yarn B**, k3 in **Yarn A**.

Row 9: K3 in **Yarn A**, p to last 3 sts in **Yarn B**, k3 in **Yarn A**.

Row 10: K3 in **Yarn A**, ssk, k to last 5 sts, k2tog in **Yarn B**, k in **Yarn A** – 33 sts.

Rows 11-34: Repeat **Rows 9-10** a further 12 times – 9 sts.

Row 35: Repeat **Row 9**.

Continue in **Yarn A** only.

Row 36: K3, CDD, k3 – 7 sts.

Row 37: K.

Row 38: K2, CDD, k2 – 5 sts.

Row 39: K1, CDD, k1 – 3 sts.

Row 40: CDD.

Break off yarn and pull through remaining st.

Finishing

- Block flags (see Finishing: Blocking) and lie flat to dry, shaping to measurements provided.

- Weave in all ends.

- Using **Yarn B**, make a tassel and attach to the bottom of the flag (see Finishing: Making a tassel).

Tutorial 19: Intarsia

Intarsia uses different coloured yarns over a knitted fabric by interlocking, or twisting, the strands of yarn at the joins.

Some intarsia projects require lots of small amounts of yarn. You can wind yarn onto bobbins or make a few small balls for each colour. For this bunting you will only need to use **Yarn A** in two separate sections and this can be done by using both ends of the yarn from the same ball.

1. When you come to the part that is worked in a different colour, join the new colour by working the first stitch with the new yarn (image 1). Continue working in this yarn until you need to change colour again (image 2). Join the new length of yarn in the same way (image 3).

2. Work to the end of the row.

3. Turn your work and work to the point where you have two colours attached to the knitting. When you pick up the new colour twist it securely around the old colour on the wrong side of the work before working the first stitch (image 4).

4. Continue working to the end of the row, twisting the yarns on the wrong side of the work as you change colour.

5. Continue working the pattern, always twisting the yarns securely on the wrong side of the work for each colour change. Move your yarns around as needed so that they don't tangle (image 5).

6. As you weave in ends, secure any holes that are left from the initial colour changes.

1.

2.

3.

4.

5.

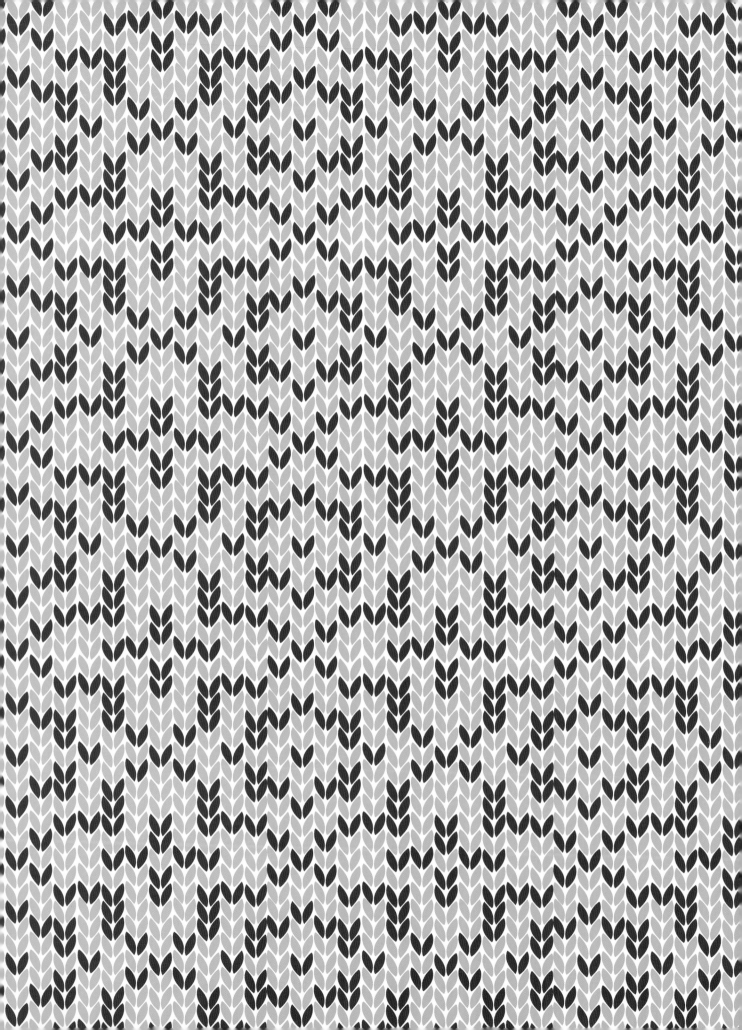

Double Knitting

Reversible Cowl

Double knitted fabric is warm and reversible so it's an ideal technique for knitting a cowl. Both sides of the knitting are worked at the same time and the yarn is moved backwards and forwards as you knit the two different layers. This cowl has a detailed and delicate pattern all over. As with many colourwork patterns a high contrast between the colours would make the pattern stand out strongly, and a low contrast would obscure the pattern. I've used two colours that contrast a reasonable amount so that the colourwork pattern is visible but subtle.

You will need

Yarn

Vivacious DK (100% merino wool), 230m/251yds per 100g skein, in the following shades:

- **Yarn A:** Copper Tones (802); 1 skein
- **Yarn B:** Sea Glass (826); 1 skein

Needles and Accessories

- Pair of 4mm (US 6/UK 8) needles or size needed to achieve correct tension
- 10 (16) stitch markers (optional)

Sizes

There are two size options:

Size 1: A short, high cowl

Size 2: A long, shallow cowl to wear long or loop over twice

- **Circumference:** 60 (96)cm/23 (38)in
- **Width:** 20 (16)cm/8 (6)in

Skills

Casting on, knit, purl, knitting in the round, increasing, decreasing, reading a chart, casting off

Tension

20 sts and 25 rows to 10 x 10cm/4 x 4in over pattern, using 4mm needles, after washing and blocking

Pattern

Using **Yarn A**, cast on 120 (192) sts and join in the round, taking care not to twist sts (see Advanced Knitting Techniques: Circular knitting). Before you begin, read the double knitting tutorial (see Tutorial 20: Double knitting).

Edge

Round 1: Knit.

Round 2: Kfb to end – 240 (384) sts.

Body

Join **Yarn B**.

Round 1: Reading chart from right to left, repeat the 12 sts of **Row 1** of the chart, 10 (16) times. Note that each square represents 2 sts. If required, place a stitch marker after every 24 sts for easier reference to the chart.

Rounds 2-12: Continue to work from chart as set until all 12 rounds have been completed.

Repeat **Rounds 1-12** twice more.

For Size 1 only:

Repeat **Rounds 1-12** once more.

Both sizes:

Repeat **Row 1** of the chart once more.

Edge

Continue in **Yarn A** only.

Round 1: (K1, p1) to end.

Cast off loosely as follows:

Ssk, (ssk, pass first st over the second st worked) to end.

Finishing

- Block cowl (see Finishing: Blocking) and lie flat to dry, shaping to measurements provided.

- Weave in all ends.

Cowl Chart

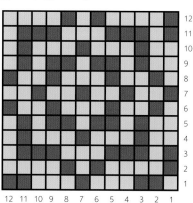

12 11 10 9 8 7 6 5 4 3 2 1

Remember that each square of the chart represents working two stitches

▢ Holding both yarns in back, k1 with Yarn B. Move both yarns to front and p1 with Yarn A.

▨ Holding both yarns in back, k1 with Yarn A. Move both yarns to front and p1 with Yarn B.

Tutorial 20: Double knitting

Double knitting is a way of making a reversible double-sided fabric by knitting two layers at once.

When working double knitting, you will need to have double the number of stitches that you normally would to make a knitted item that is the same dimensions but double the thickness. Half of the stitches will make one side and the other half will make the other side.

For this cowl pattern, when one stitch is worked in **Yarn A** the next stitch is worked in **Yarn B** and vice versa. Every other stitch is purled and you need to ensure that you are bringing both strands of yarn to the correct side of the work as you make each stitch. The directions below refer to the first few stitches from the Cowl colourwork chart.

Square 1 of colourwork chart

1. Holding both yarns in back, K1 with **Yarn B** (image 1).

2. Bring both yarns to front (image 2).

3. P1 with **Yarn A** (image 3).

Square 2 of colourwork chart

1. Take both yarns to back (image 4).

2. K1 with **Yarn A** (image 5).

3. Bring both yarns forward.

4. P1 with **Yarn B** (image 6).

5. Continue working from the chart in this way working 2 stitches for every square on the chart.

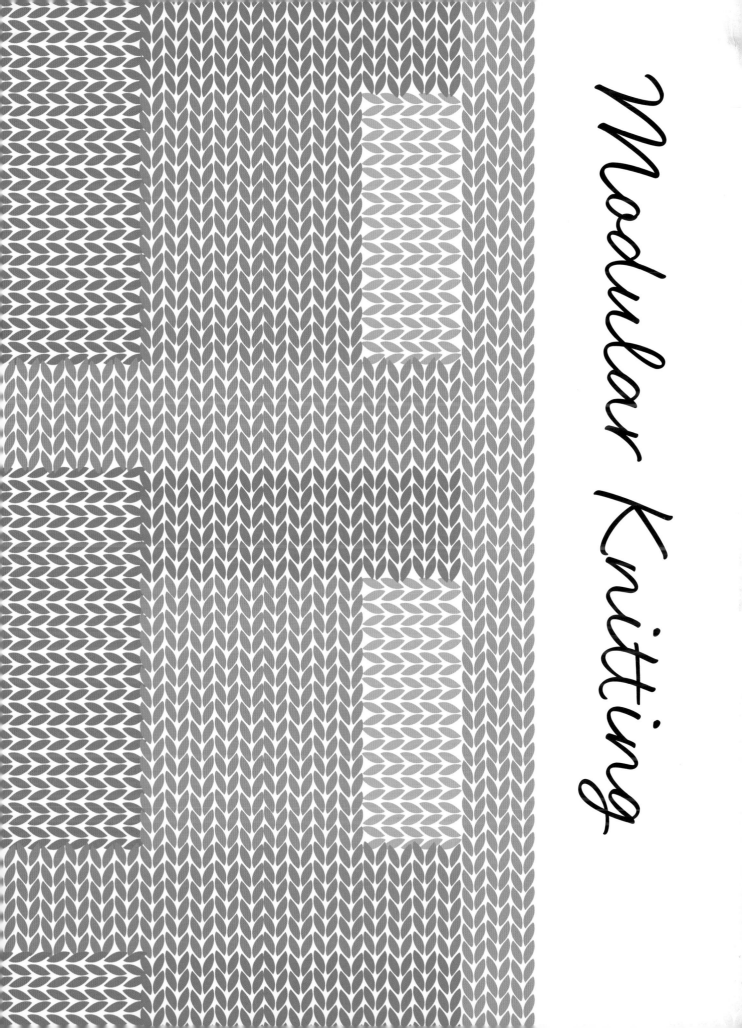

Modular Knitting

Log Cabin Blanket

This blanket is made from nine log cabin squares sewn together and finished with a picked up border. Each log cabin square is composed of a knitted square with rectangles picked up along the edge and knitted on. The construction method is enhanced by using different colours for each module. Log cabin blankets are bold, geometric designs that would look effective in many different colour schemes. Each knitted section is large and distinct enough that you don't really need to restrict your colour choices by contrast or anything else. Hand-dyed yarns could look lovely in a log cabin blanket. I've opted for a pastel colour scheme using colours that are gentle but still vibrant.

You will need

Yarn

Cascade 220 Heathers Worsted (100% wool), 201m/220yds per 100g skein, in the following shades:

- **Yarn A:** Summer Sky Heather (9452); 1 skein
- **Yarn B:** Dune Heather (9460); 1 skein
- **Yarn C:** Peony Pink (2449); 1 skein
- **Yarn D:** Purple Tourmaline (9641); 1 skein
- **Yarn E:** Aspen Heather (8011); 1 skein
- **Yarn F:** Greystone Heather (9491); 1 skein

Needles and Accessories

- Pair of 5mm (US 8/UK 6) needles or size needed to achieve correct tension
- A 5mm (US 8/UK 6) long circular needle or size needed to achieve correct tension for working the borders

Size

One size: 84 x 84cm/33 x 33in

Skills

Casting on, knit, picking up sts, casting off

Tension

15 sts and 30 rows to 10 x 10cm/4 x 4in over garter stitch, using 5mm needles, after washing and blocking

Pattern

Make a total of 9 log cabin squares, referring to Tutorial 21: Log cabin squares before you begin, and use the diagram below as a guide for the colour order, if desired.

Centre Square

Using **Yarn A**, cast on 20 sts.

Rows 1-40: K.

Cast off all sts, except the final st and leave this on the needle – 1 st.

Rotate work clockwise.

Strip 1

Switch to **Yarn B**.

Knit the st remaining on the needle. Pick up a further 19 sts along the side of the centre square – 20 sts.

Rows 1-19: K.

Cast off all sts except the final st and leave this on the needle – 1 st.

Rotate work clockwise.

Strip 2

Switch to **Yarn C**.

Knit the st remaining on the needle. Pick up a further 9 sts along the side of strip 1, pick up 20 sts along the centre square – 30 sts.

Rows 1-19: K.

Cast off all sts except the final st and leave this on the needle – 1 st.

Rotate work clockwise.

Strip 3

Switch to **Yarn D** and work as given for Strip 2.

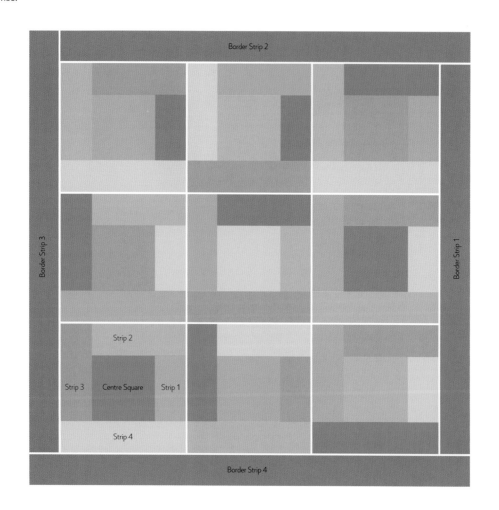

Strip 4

Switch to **Yarn E**.

Knit the st remaining on the needle. Pick up a further 9 sts along the side of the strip 3, pick up 20 sts along the centre square, pick up 10 sts along the edge of strip 1 – 40 sts.

Rows 1-19: K.

Cast off all sts.

Log Cabin Squares

Make eight further log cabin squares, following the instructions above but using the yarn colours for each section in a different order. Use photos and diagram as a guide if desired.

Arrange the total of nine squares as illustrated by photos and diagram and join them together using mattress stitch (see Finishing: Mattress stitch).

Border

The border uses the same technique as the log cabin squares. You will pick up stitches across the long edges of the blanket and then pick up additional stitches along the edges of the border that have already been worked. Note that the last stitch remaining after casting off a strip will count as the first picked up stitch for the next strip.

Pick up the correct number of stitches for each part of the blanket that you come to, in whatever order you come to them. Use photos and diagram as a guide if desired.

For each part of the border pick up and knit the following number of stitches for each part of the log cabin squares; 10 sts along every short edge of the strips, 20 sts along the edges of strip 1, 30 sts along the long edges of strips 2 and 3, and 40 sts along the long edges of strip 4. There will be a total of 40 sts picked up along the edge of each log cabin square.

In addition, pick up and knit 5 sts along any of the border edges that have already been worked.

Border Strip 1

Using **Yarn F**, pick up and knit a total of 120 sts along the edge of the blanket.

Rows 1-9: K.

Cast off all sts except the final st and leave this on the needle – 1 st.

Rotate work clockwise.

Border Strip 2

Knit the st remaining on the needle. Pick up a further 4 sts along the side of border strip 1, pick up 120 sts along the edge of the blanket – 125 sts.

Rows 1-9: K.

Cast off all sts except the final st and leave this on the needle – 1 st.

Rotate work clockwise.

Border Strip 3

Work as given for Border Strip 2.

Border Strip 4

Knit the st remaining on the needle. Pick up a further 4 sts along the side of border strip 1, pick up 120 sts along the edge of the blanket, pick up 5 sts along the side of border strip 1 – 130 sts.

Rows 1-9: K.

Cast off all sts.

Finishing

- Block blanket (see Finishing: Blocking) and lie flat to dry, shaping to measurements provided.

- Weave in all ends.

Tutorial 21: Log cabin square

Log cabin squares are a simple modular design composed of strips of knitting. These strips are joined as you work, by picking up stitches. Each square can then be joined together by seaming to make a larger item, such as this blanket.

1. Knit the centre square and cast off all but the final stitch (image 1).

2. Using the new colour yarn, knit the last stitch on the needle. Turn the work and pick up the required number of stitches along the edge of the knitting (image 2). Using the garter stitch bumps as a guide, you can pick up your stitches in between each bump and make sure that you insert your needle under two strands of yarn, for a neat finish.

3. Repeat **Step 2** (image 3).

4. Repeat **Step 2** twice more (image 4).

5. Cast off all stitches to complete the square (image 5).

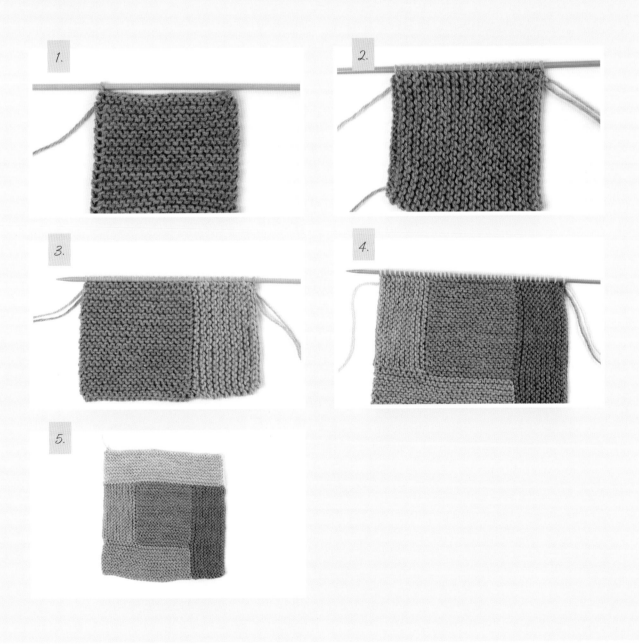

Entrelac

Variegated Wrap

Entrelac is a fun way to play with colour. It's not strictly speaking a colourwork technique, but rather a construction method that works well with use of colour. Entrelac works well with multicoloured yarns where each colour blends into another over a long length of yarn. This is ideal for when you want to use many colours but would rather have them already put together in a palette that works. I've used a lovely luxury yarn with silk and wool in a bright and beautiful colour combination. There are more restrained colour combinations available and there are many other yarn options that have a similar effect.

You will need

Yarn

♦ Noro Silk Garden Aran (45% silk, 45% mohair, 10% wool), 100m/109yds per 50g ball, in shade Rainbow (87); 6 balls

Needles and Accessories

♦ Pair of 5mm (US 8/UK 6) needles or size needed to achieve correct tension

Size

One size: 130 x 45cm/51 x 17¾in

Skills

Casting on, knit, purl, increasing, decreasing, picking up sts, casting off

Tension

16 sts and 22 rows to 10 x 10cm/4 x 4in over st st, using 5mm needles, after washing and blocking

Pattern

Cast on 40 sts. Read through Tutorial 22: Entrelac knitting, before starting your wrap.

Foundation Triangles

Row 1 (RS): K2, turn.

Row 2 (WS): P2, turn.

Row 3: K3, turn.

Row 4: P3, turn.

Row 5: K4, turn.

Row 6: P4, turn.

Row 7: K5, turn.

Row 8: P5, turn.

Row 9: K6, turn.

Row 10: P6, turn.

Row 11: K7, turn.

Row 12: P7, turn.

Row 13: K8.

This completes the first triangle.

Repeat **Rows 1-13** 4 times more, to complete five triangles in total.

Tier 1

This tier consists of a triangle at the right edge, four blocks, and a triangle at the left edge.

Left Side Triangle

Row 1 (WS): P2, turn.

Row 2 (RS): K1, m1, k1, turn.

Row 3: P2, p2tog, turn.

Row 4: K2, m1, k1, turn.

Row 5: P3, p2tog, turn.

Row 6: K3, m1, k1, turn.

Row 7: P4, p2tog, turn.

Row 8: K4, m1, k1, turn.

Row 9: P5, p2tog, turn.

Row 10: K5, m1, k1, turn.

Row 11: P6, p2tog, turn.

Row 12: K6, m1, k1, turn.

Row 13: P7, k2tog.

This completes the left edge triangle.

Blocks

With WS facing, pick up and purl 8 sts along the edge of the next triangle or block, turn.

Row 1 (RS): K8, turn.

Row 2 (WS): P7, p2tog, turn.

Rows 3-14: Repeat **Rows 1-2** 6 times more.

Row 15: Repeat **Row 1**.

Row 16: P7, p2tog.

Repeat **Rows 1-16** 3 times more, completing four blocks in total.

Right Side Triangle

With WS, pick up and purl 8 sts along the edge of the next triangle or block, turn.

Row 1 (RS): K8, turn.

Row 2 (WS): P6, p2tog, turn.

Row 3: K7, turn.

Row 4: P5, p2tog, turn.

Row 5: K6, turn.

Row 6: P4, p2tog, turn.

Row 7: K5, turn.

Row 8: P3, p2tog, turn.

Row 9: K4, turn.

Row 10: P2, p2tog, turn.

Row 11: K3, turn.

Row 12: P1, p2tog, turn.

Row 13: K2, turn.

Row 14: P2tog, turn and slip last st to the right needle.

This completes the second side triangle.

Tier 2

This tier consists of five blocks.

With RS facing and 1 st on the right needle, pick up and knit 7 sts along the edge of the next triangle or block, turn.

Note: The st remaining on the needle counts as your first st, so you only need to pick up and knit 7 sts to have 8 sts for the first block. Pick up 8 sts for all remaining blocks.

Row 1 (WS): P8, turn.

Row 2 (RS): K7, ssk, turn.

Rows 3-14: Repeat **Rows 1-2** 6 times more.

Row 15: Repeat **Row 1**.

Row 16: K7, ssk.

Repeat **Rows 1-16** 3 times more, completing four blocks in total.

Repeat all instructions for Tiers 1 and 2 a further 13 times.

Complete Tier 1 once more.

Top Triangles

With RS facing, pick up and knit 7 sts along the edge of the next triangle or block, turn.

Note: The st remaining on the needle counts as your first st, so you only need to pick up and knit 7 sts to have 8 sts for each top triangle.

Row 1 (WS): P8, turn.

Row 2 (RS): Ssk, k5, ssk, turn.

Row 3: P7, turn.

Row 4: Ssk, k4, ssk, turn.

Row 5: P6, turn.

Row 6: Ssk, k3, ssk, turn.

Row 7: P5, turn.

Row 8: Ssk, k2, ssk, turn.

Row 9: P4, turn.

Row 10: Ssk, k1, ssk, turn.

Row 11: P3, turn.

Row 12: Ssk, ssk, turn.

Row 13: P2, turn.

Row 14: K1, ssk, turn.

Row 15: P2, turn.

Row 16: Sl1 as if to knit with yarn in back, ssk, pass slipped st over, do not turn.

This completes the first top triangle.

Repeat **Rows 1-16** 4 times more, completing five top triangles in total.

Break off yarn and pull through remaining st.

Finishing

- Block wrap (see Finishing: Blocking) and lie flat to dry, shaping to measurements provided.

- Weave in all ends.

Tutorial 22: Entrelac knitting

Entrelac is a modular knitting technique that uses picked up stitches, short rows and simple shaping to make tiers of rectangles in a basket-weave pattern.

Foundation triangles

To make straight, neat edges the entralec pattern begins with a row of foundation triangles.

1. Start the triangle by knitting 2 stitches.

2. Turn your work and purl across the 2 stitches you just knitted.

3. Turn your work and knit across the 2 stitches you just purled, and then knit another stitch.

4. Continue working the triangle in this way until you have knitted 8 stitches.

5. Repeat **Steps 1-4** until you have completed the entire row of foundation triangles (image 1).

Tier 1

This tier is composed of a triangle at each end and blocks along the middle.

1. Start knitting a triangle on the side of the work by purling 2 stitches, then turning your work.

2. Continue working the triangle by increasing, using m1, along the outside edge of the work on RS rows. Purl 2 stitches together on WS rows to join the triangle to the section below (image 2).

3. Once the triangle is complete, all of the stitches from the section below will have been decreased and joined to the triangle, leaving the 8 stitches worked on the needle (image 3).

1.

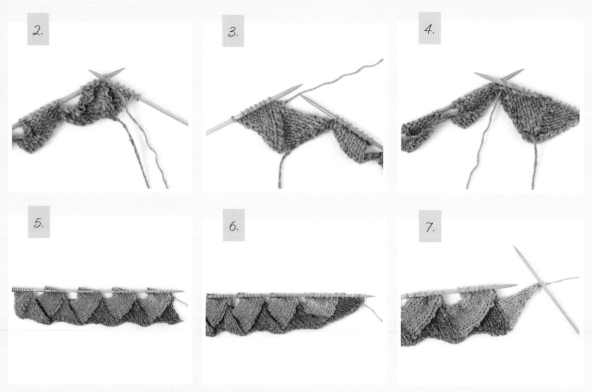

2.   3.   4.

5.   6.   7.

4. Start knitting blocks by picking up 8 stitches along the edge of the section below (image 4).

5. Continue working the blocks by knitting across the 8 stitches, then turning your work, purling 7 stitches, and then purling 2 stitches together to join the block to the section below.

6. Repeat **Steps 4-5** until you have completed the row of blocks (image 5).

7. Work a triangle at the edge of the knitting by picking up 8 stitches along the edge of the section below (image 6).

8. Complete the triangle by knitting across the stitches on RS rows and purling 2 stitches together along the outside edge of the triangle on WS rows until only 1 stitch remains (image 7).

Tier 2

This tier is composed of blocks leaning across the opposite direction to Tier 1.

1. Keep the final stitch from the previous section on the needle and continue picking up a further 7 stitches along the edge of the section below (image 8).

2. Continue working the block by purling across the stitches and working a ssk decrease on RS rows to join the block to the section below (image 9).

3. Complete all blocks to the end of the work (image 10).

Repeat Tiers 1 and 2 until the knitting reaches the desired length ending after completing a Tier 1 section.

Top triangles

Work a row of top triangles to finish the knitting with a neat edge.

1. Keep the final stitch from the previous section on the needle and continue picking up sts along the edge of the section below (image 11).

2. Work a top triangle by casting off a stitch at one end and working a ssk decrease at the other end across the section below (image 12).

3. Complete all top triangles to the end of the work (image 13).

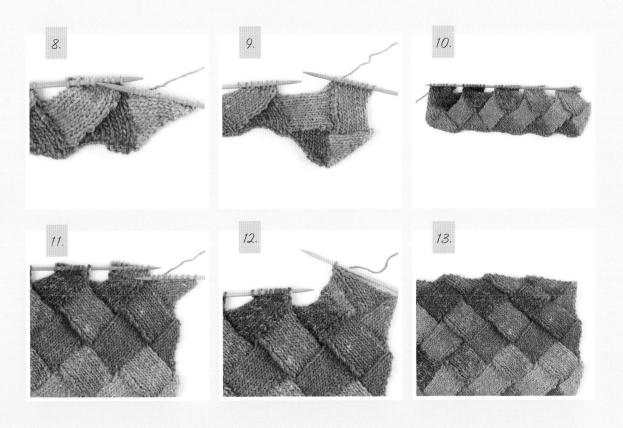

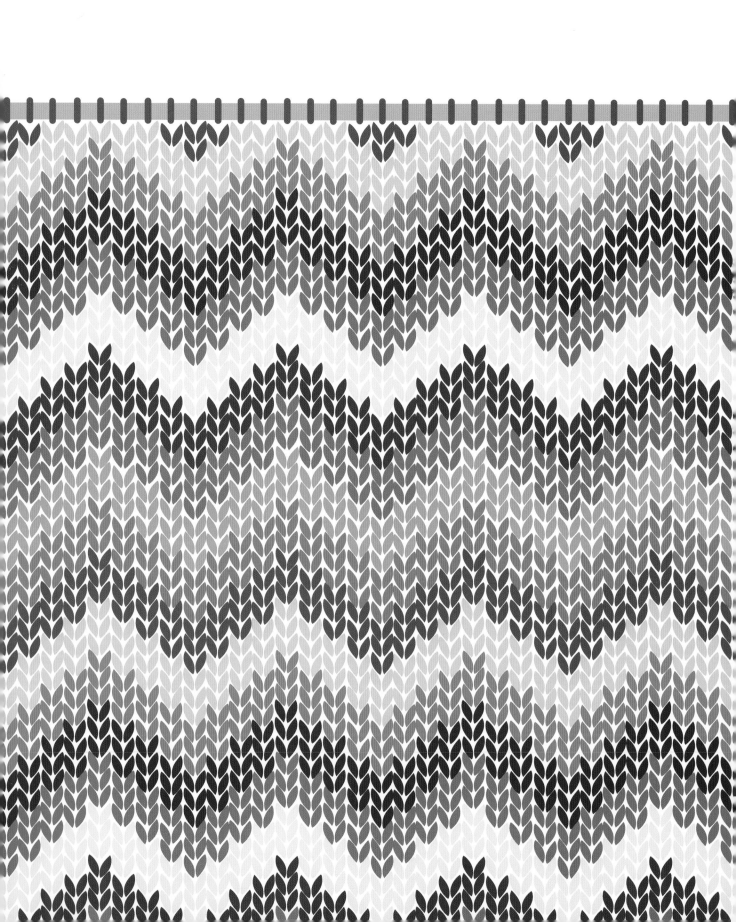

Techniques

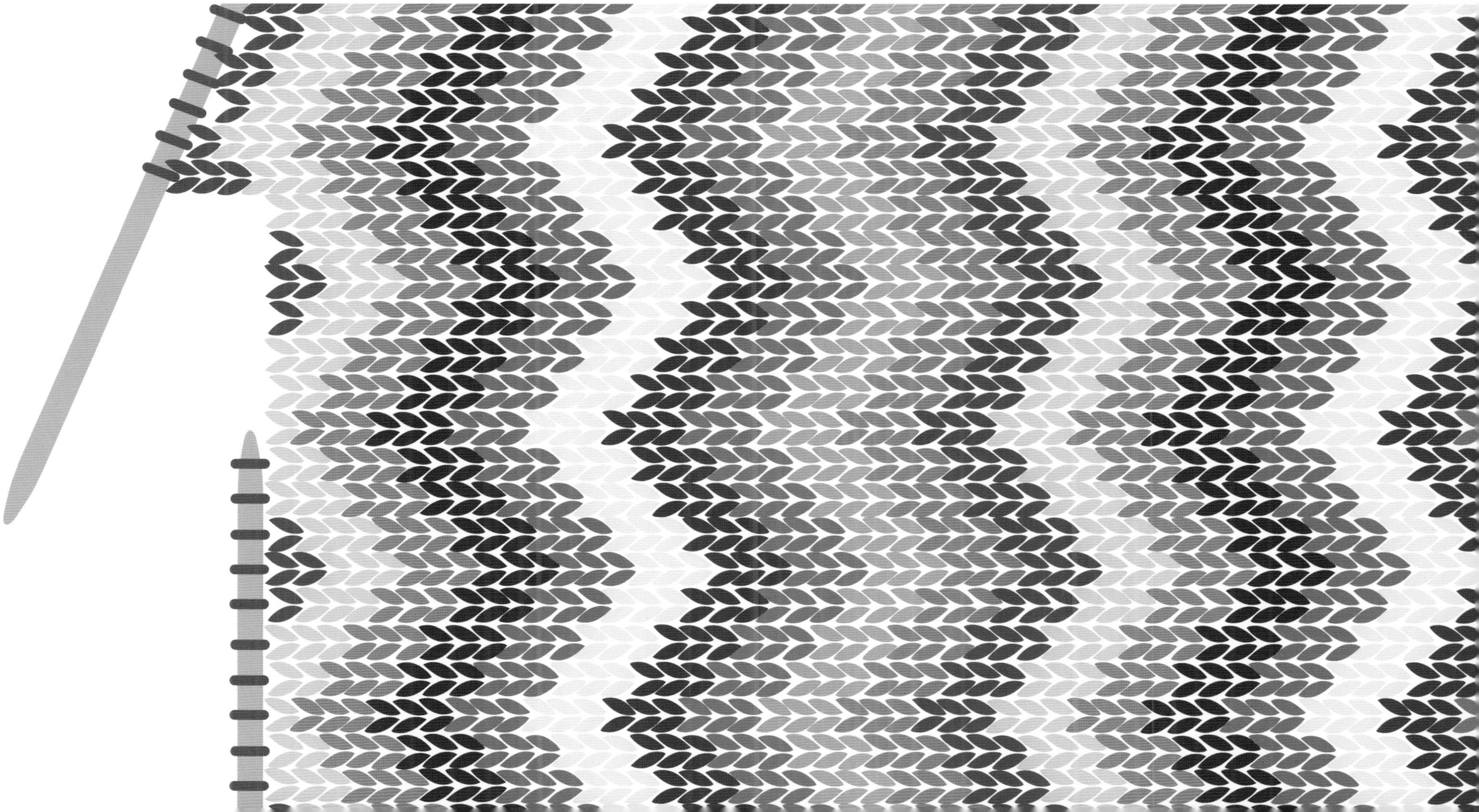

Abbreviations

- **CDD** centred double decrease
- **k** knit
- **kfb** knit into front and back of stitch
- **KYOK** knit 1, yarn over, knit 1 into the same st
- **k2tog** knit 2 sts together
- **m** marker
- **m1** make 1 st
- **m1L** make 1 left

- **m1R** make 1 right
- **p** purl
- **pm** place marker
- **p2tog** purl 2sts together
- **RS** right side
- **sl** slip
- **slm** slip marker
- **ssk** slip, slip, knit these 2 sts together

- **st(s)** stitch(es)
- **st st** stocking stitch
- **WS** wrong side
- **wyif** with yarn in front
- **wyib** with yarn in back
- **YO** yarn over
- **yrn** yarn round needle

Getting Started

Making a slip knot

These cast on methods start with a slip knot.

1. Make a loop with your yarn (image 1).

2. Using your needle, or a finger, draw another loop of yarn through the first loop (image 2).

3. Pull the ends of the yarn to fit the knot snuggly on the needle (image 3). This will form the first stitch.

1.

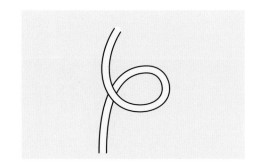

2.

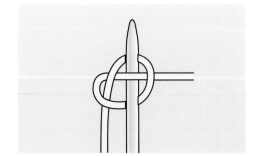

3.

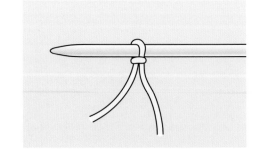

Long tail cast on

A long tail cast on makes a firm and neat cast on edge.

1. Pull a length of yarn just over three times the width of your knitting. Make a slip knot at this point and place it on your needle.

2. Hold the lengths of yarn looped over your thumb and index finger, secured in the palm of your hand (image 4).

3. Insert the needle through the loop around your thumb and through the front strand of the loop over your index finger (image 5).

4. Draw the yarn from the index finger through the loop over your thumb (image 6). Let the loop slide off your thumb and form the base of the stitch on the needle (image 7).

5. Form a new loop around your thumb and repeat the steps until you have the required number of stitches.

Knitted cast on

A knitted cast on makes a loose edge with some stretch.

1. Leaving an end at least 10cm/4in long, make a slip knot and place it on your left needle (image 8).

2. Insert your right needle tip into the slip knot and wrap the working yarn (the length of yarn attached to the ball) around the right needle tip.

3. Draw the yarn through the stitch (image 9) and place it on to the left needle (image 10).

4. Repeat these steps until you have made the number of stitches required (image 11).

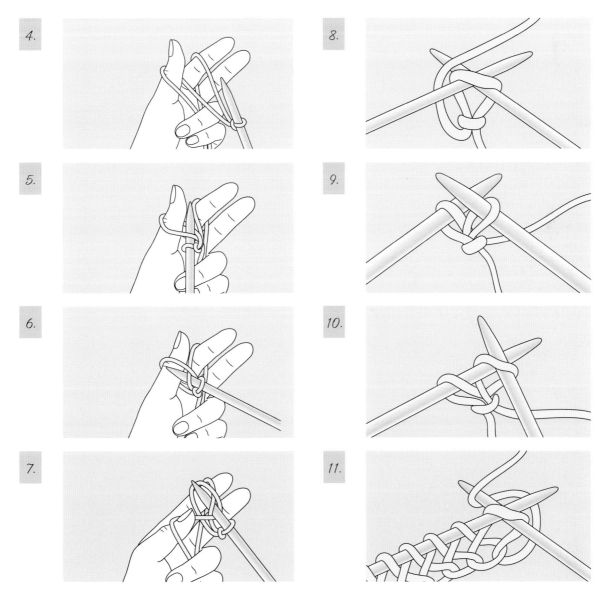

4.

5.

6.

7.

8.

9.

10.

11.

Alternating cable cast on

An alternating cable cast on makes a neat edge for ribbed knitting.

1. Leaving an end at least 10cm/4in long, make a slip knot and place it on your left needle.

2. Make one stitch in the same way as a knitted cast on (image 12) (see Knitted Cast On).

3. The next stitch is made purlwise. Insert your right needle between the last two stitches from back to front. Wrap the yarn around the right needle tip (image 13), draw it through and place it onto the left needle.

4. The next stitch is made knitwise. Insert your right needle between the last two stitches from front to back (image 14). Wrap the yarn around the right needle tip, draw it through and place it on the left needle.

5. Repeat the last two steps until you have made the number of stitches required.

Cast off

Casting off, or binding off, creates a neat and secure edge to finish your work.

1. Knit two stitches (see Knit Stitch).

2. Insert the tip of your left needle into the bottom stitch on the right needle (image 15) and pass it over the second stitch and off the right needle (image 16 and image 17).

3. Knit another stitch so that you have two stitches on the needle again.

4. Repeat the last two steps until one stitch remains (if you are casting off all stitches).

5. Cut the working yarn and draw it through the final stitch, pulling it tight to secure it.

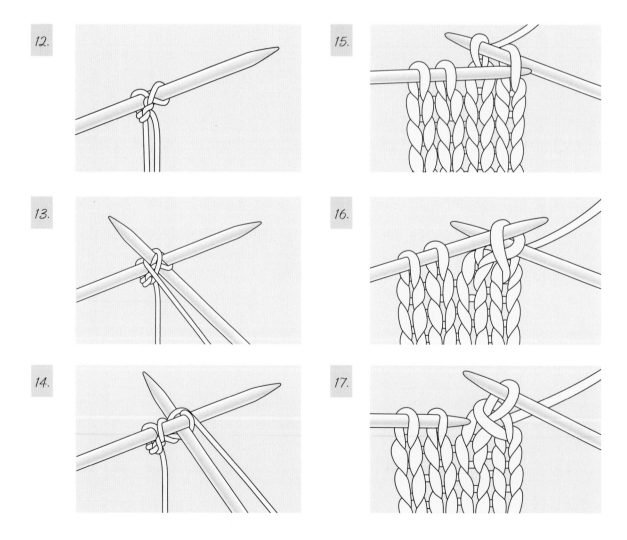

12.

13.

14.

15.

16.

17.

Knit and Purl Stitches

Knit stitch

The knit stitch is the simplest stitch to make and forms the basis for most other knitted techniques. A knit stitch makes a flat 'V' on the side of the knitting facing you, and a 'bump' on the opposite side.

1. Insert the tip of the right needle, from front to back, into the first stitch on the left needle (image 1a and image 1b).

2. Wrap the yarn around the tip of the right needle (image 2a and image 2b).

3. Draw the yarn through the stitch (image 3a and image 3b).

4. Slip the stitch off of the left needle (image 4a and image 4b).

English method

Continental method

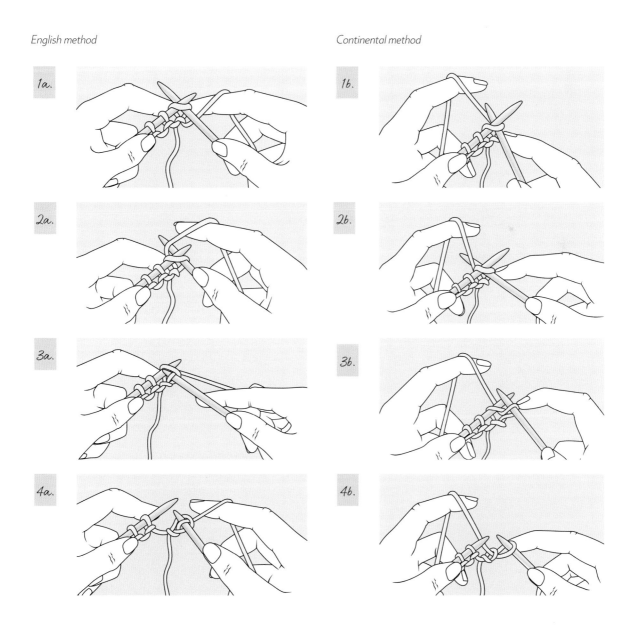

Purl stitch

The purl stitch is like a backwards knit stitch. It is worked in a similar way to the knit stitch. However, by inserting the right needle into the stitch from the opposite direction, the flat 'V' of the stitch will be at the back of the work and the 'bump', sometimes called a 'purl bump', will be facing you.

1. Insert the tip of the right needle, from back to front, into the first stitch on the left needle (image 5a and image 5b).

2. Wrap the yarn around the tip of the right needle (image 6a and image 6b).

3. Draw the yarn through the stitch (image 7a and image 7b).

4. Slip the stitch off of the left needle (image 8a and image 8b).

English method   *Continental method*

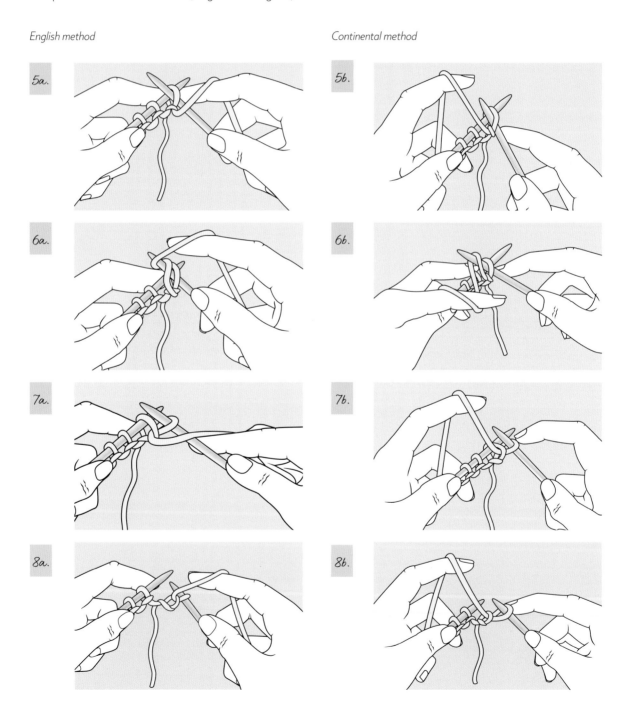

Basic Knitting Techniques

Increase M1L

The m1L increase will make a left-leaning stitch in your knitting between two stitches.

1. Insert the left needle, from front to back, under the horizontal bar of yarn between the stitches on each needle (image 1).

2. Knit into the back of the bar of yarn (image 2). This will avoid a hole under the increase by twisting the bar of yarn.

Increase M1R

The m1R increase will make a right-leaning stitch in your knitting between two stitches.

1. Insert the left needle, from back to front, under the horizontal bar of yarn between the stitches on each needle (image 3).

2. Knit into the front of the bar of yarn (image 4). This will avoid a hole under the increase by twisting the bar of yarn.

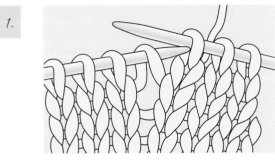

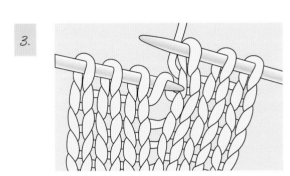

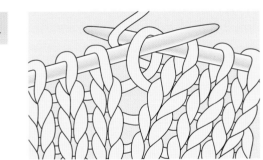

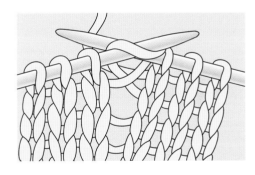

Increase (or make an eyelet) yarn over

A yarn over increase will make an extra stitch and form a small hole under the new stitch that can be used as a decorative feature or a buttonhole.

Wrap the yarn over the needle. The loop of yarn that is left over the needle when you work the next stitch will be worked as a stitch on the following row (or round) (image 5).

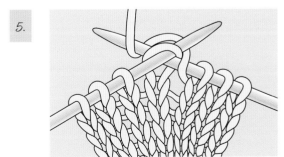

Increase double increase, KYOK (K1, YO, K1)

This increase will form two extra stitches from one stitch.

1. Knit into the stitch without slipping it off the left needle (image 6).

2. Wrap the yarn over the right needle (image 7) and knit into the same stitch on the left needle again, this time letting it slip from the left needle.

Decrease SSK

The ssk decrease forms a left-leaning increase. It's often used to match and mirror the k2tog decrease. Slipping the stitches before knitting them together twists the stitches so that they will lean to the left.

1. Slip the next two stitches knitwise (inserting the right needle as though you were going to knit them) one by one onto the right needle (image 8).

2. Insert the tip of the left needle into the front loops of both stitches (image 9) and knit them together.

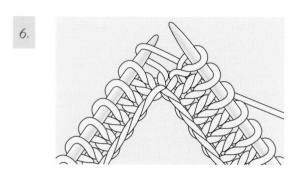

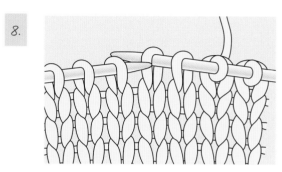

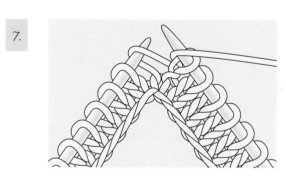

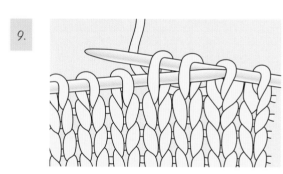

Decrease K2tog

Knitting two stitches together makes a right-leaning decrease.

Insert right needle from front to back into both of the next two stitches on the left needle (image 10). Knit the stitches together, slipping both from the needle at once.

Decrease P2tog

Purling two stitches together forms a decrease within a purl row.

Insert the right needle from back to front into the next two stitches on the left needle (image 11). Purl the stitches together, slipping both from the needle at once.

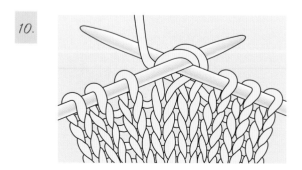

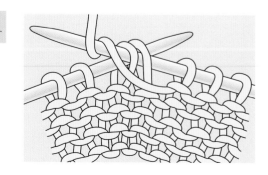

Centred double decrease CDD

The centred double decrease (CDD) decreases two stitches and allows the centre stitch of the three stitches worked to lie at the front of the decrease for a neat finish.

1. Slip the next two stitches onto the right needle together knitwise. This will twist the stitches so that one crosses over the other (image 12).

2. Knit the next stitch and then pass both of the slipped stitches over the stitch that you have just knitted, allowing them to slide off both needles (image 13).

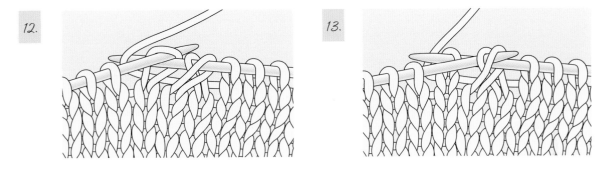

Picking up stitches

Stitches can be picked up across the edges of knitting forming a new row of knitting that is attached to another knitted piece.

1. Insert your needle through the edge of the knitting where you would like to make a stitch (image 14).

2. Wrap the yarn over the tip of the needle (image 15) and pull a loop of yarn through to the front of the knitting (image 16).

3. Repeat the last two steps evenly along the edge of the fabric until you have the desired number of stitches (image 17).

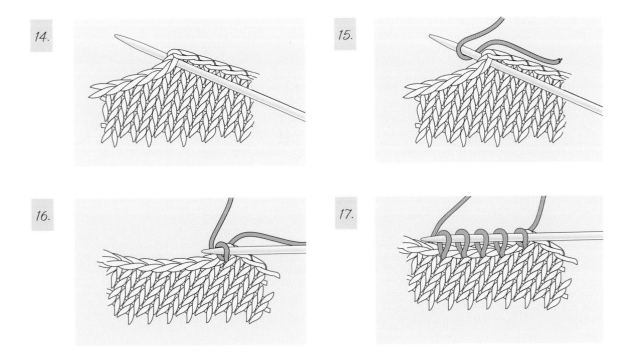

Advanced Knitting Techniques

Circular knitting

Circular knitting, or knitting in the round, creates a seamless tube of fabric. This method can be worked on double-pointed needles (DPNS) or a circular knitting needle (see Yarn and Tools).

Circular needles

Make sure the circular needle you choose is long enough to hold the required number of stitches for your pattern, but remember that the stitches need to stretch all the way around the cord to be able to knit the round (unless you are using the the magic loop technique).

Cast on the stitches and spread them along the length of the circular needle, making sure that the stitches are not twisted. It's useful to mark the first stitch with a stitch marker to keep track of the beginning of the round.

You can still create a flat piece of knitting with knit and purl rows using circular needles. Simply turn the work at the end of every row and swap the needles between hands. This is useful for large numbers of stitches, such as blankets and shawls.

Magic loop

The magic loop method can be used for working small circumferences in the round.

Cast on the required number of stitches and divide them in half equally, placing half on one needle and the rest on the cord. Pull a length of cord at roughly halfway through your cast on stitches and make sure the stitches are not twisted.

Arrange your needle so that the first stitch you cast on is at the tip of your left needle with half the stitches following it and the other half of your stitches at the centre of the cord. The right needle should be empty of stitches.

Without twisting the stitches, arrange your work so that the working yarn meets your first stitch to be worked. Place a stitch marker to mark the beginning/end of the round if desired and knit the stitches from the left-hand needle, using the right-hand needle, pulling tightly on the yarn for the first few stitches to make sure the round joins seamlessly and there are no loose stitches.

Next, pull out the right-hand needle, leaving its stitches on the cord so you can use it to knit off the left-hand needle. Continue for the required length.

Double-pointed needles

These are available in sets of four or five. First, cast on your stitches onto one DPN, then divide them evenly between three or four DPNS by slipping the stitches purlwise. Reserve one DPN to start knitting with.

As with circular needles, make sure that the cast-on row is not twisted before you start knitting and use a stitch marker to identify the first stitch. Make sure that the right side of your work is facing you.

When you are knitting, you will need to make sure that you keep the tension of the stitches even throughout. To do this, when you move from one DPN to the next, always pull the yarn firmly when knitting the first stitch at the change-over point. This is important because if you have lots of loose stitches at the same point in your rows of knitting, it will look like a ladder and will be noticeable.

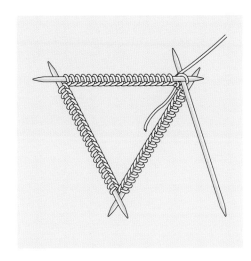

3.

Afterthought heel and thumb

In theory an afterthought heel or thumb can be worked anywhere in your knitting, however in many patterns the placement will be reserved with scrap yarn. When the scrap yarn is removed, the picked up stitches can be knitted to form a neat edge for a thumb opening or a heel.

1. Using DPNS (or your prefered method for knitting small circumferences in the round) insert your needle into the middle of each stitch either side of your scrap yarn (image 4 and image 5).

2. Remove the scrap yarn (image 6).

3. Divide the stitches over your needles ready to start knitting in the round (image 7). Join your yarn and follow the pattern instructions to continue your work.

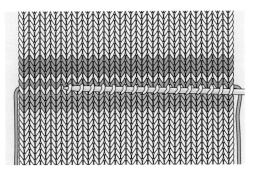

4.

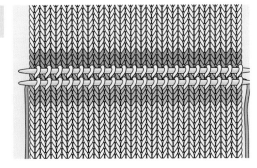

5.

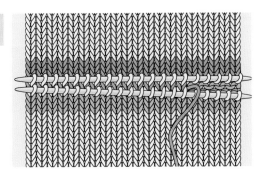

6.

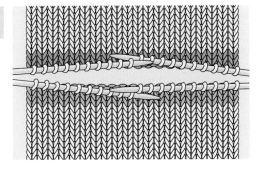

7.

Kitchener stitch

Kitchener stitch, or grafting, is a neat way to close your knitted stitches without making a seam. This method is particularly popular to close the toes, and sometimes heels, in socks.

Arrange your knitting so that the two rows to be grafted closed are on two needles (or two ends of a circular needle) held together with one in front of the other.

Thread the end of your yarn (or a new length of yarn) onto a blunt tapestry needle.

Insert the tapestry needle into the first stitch on the front needle from back to front, as if to purl the stitch (image 8). Leave the stitch on the knitting needle and draw the yarn through.

Insert the tapestry needle into the first stitch on the back needle from front to back, as if to knit the stitch (image 9). Leave the stitch on the knitting needle and draw the yarn through.

1. Insert the tapestry needle into the first stitch of the front needle from front to back, as if to knit the stitch (image 10). Slip the stitch off of the needle and draw the yarn through.

2. Insert the tapestry needle into the next stitch on the front needle from back to front, as if the purl the stitch (image 11). Leave the stitch on the knitting needle and draw the yarn through.

3. Insert the tapestry needle into the first stitch on the back needle from back to front, as if to purl the stitch (image 12). Slip the stitch off of the needle and draw the yarn through.

4. Insert the tapestry needle into the next stitch on the back needle from front to back as if to knit the stitch. Leave the stitch on the knitting needle and draw the yarn through.

Repeat **Steps 1-4** to graft the two sets of stitches together (image 13). When you reach the last two stitches, repeat **Step 1** then **Step 4**.

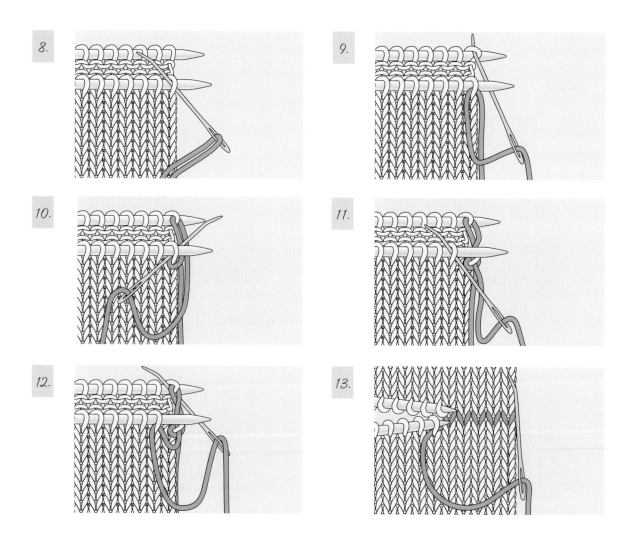

Finishing

Blocking

Blocking is recommended for finishing most knitting projects. The process of wetting and shaping your knitting will improve its appearance by enhancing the shape, smoothing the tension, setting the stitches and allowing the yarn to bloom into a soft, knitted fabric.

1. Fill a basin or bowl with cold or lukewarm water (check the ball band for temperature instructions). If desired you can add a small amount of detergent (such as a wool wash or a mild shampoo).

2. Place your knitting into the water to wet it completely and leave to soak for approximately 20 minutes.

3. Lift your fabric out of the basin or bowl and at the same time very carefully squeeze out the excess water. Take care when lifting out of the water when soaking wet, as your knitting may stretch. Do not wring, otherwise you could damage your fabric.

4. Carefully lay your work onto a towel, then starting at one end, loosely roll up the towel. Lightly apply pressure to squeeze out the excess water.

5. Unroll the towel, then place your work onto a flat surface. Pin to shape with right side uppermost, according to your measurements, using rust-proof pins or blocking pins. Alternatively socks and accessories can be blocked on forms such as sock blockers.

6. Leave to dry completely before removing the pins.

Mattress stitch

This stitch makes an invisible and flexible seam, neatly attaching two pieces of knitting together. Mattress stitch is worked with the right sides of the knitting facing so it's easier to control the finished appearance of your seam.

1. Place your two pieces of knitting with right side uppermost. Thread the tail end of yarn from one piece onto a wool needle. Insert the needle up through the first cast on or cast off stitch on opposite piece, from back to front. Then insert needle up through the corner stitch on the first piece, from back to front. Pull yarn through and pull tight to bring the edges together.

2. Take the needle across to the opposite edge again and insert it, from the front, under the horizontal bar in the middle of the outer row of stitches (image 1).

Repeat **Step 2**, working back and forth across each side, gently pulling the yarn through to close the seam (image 2). Make sure you always work along a straight line of stitches for a perfect finish.

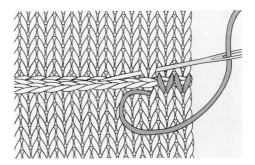

1.

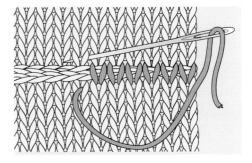

2.

Making a pompom

1. Cut 2 circular pieces of card to the size of pompom required. Cut a smaller hole in the centre of each piece. Wrap yarn around the card, taking it through the centre (image 3), until the centre hole is filled. The more you wrap, the fuller the pompom will be.

2. Use a sharp pair of scissors to cut through the wrapped yarn (image 4).

3. Thread a length of yarn between the card circles and tie tightly (image 5). Carefully remove the cardboard, give your pompom a good shake and trim the ends to make a rounded shape.

You can also buy a pompom maker. These come in different sizes and will include instructions on how to use them.

Making a tassel

1. Cut a piece of card to length of tassel required. Wrap yarn around the card, approximately 25-30 times.

2. Thread a length of yarn underneath the top folded edge and tie tightly (image 6).

3. Use a sharp pair of scissors to cut through the wrapped yarn at the opposite end (image 7).

4. Tie a second length of yarn approximately 2cm/¾in below the top to create a bulb shape, then trim the loose end straight (image 8).

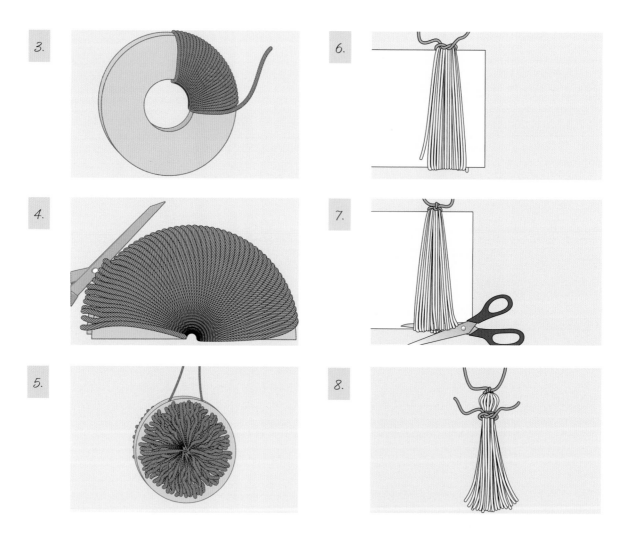

3.

4.

5.

6.

7.

8.

Suppliers

Baa Ram Ewe www.baaramewe.co.uk

Knit with Attitude www.knitwithattitude.com

Love Knitting www.loveknitting.com

Loop www.loopknittingshop.com

SewandSo www.sewandso.co.uk

WEBS www.yarn.com

Wool on the Exe www.woolontheexe.com

Wool Warehouse www.woolwarehouse.co.uk

Thanks

This book has been a joy to write and I'm grateful to all who made it possible.

A huge thank you to everyone who has followed my design work or knitted one of my patterns; your support is so valuable and very much appreciated.

Thank you to the team at F&W Media; Sarah for making this book happen, Jeni and Lynne for pulling it all together and ensuring that everything adds up and makes sense, Sam for making the book look great, Jason for brilliant photography skills, and Kang for creating the gorgeous illustrations.

Thank you to Belinda of the Knitting Hotel, Dawlish, for making us feel welcome at the photo shoot.

Thank you to all of my friends and family who have encouraged and supported me, had confidence in me and tolerated my obsession with this project! And an extra special thank you to my children, Bonnie, Mabel and Erik xxx

About the Author

Ella has always loved knitting and began designing a few years after starting a family. She now designs for magazines and yarn companies from her home in Devon, UK, where she lives with her husband, three children, two cats and one dog. You can find her online at:

Website: bombella.co.uk

Instagram: instagram.com/bombellaella

Ravelry: ravelry.com/designers/ella-austin

Index

A SEWANDSO BOOK
© F&W Media International, Ltd 2019

SewandSo is an imprint of F&W Media International, Ltd
Pynes Hill Court, Pynes Hill, Exeter, EX2 5AZ, UK

F&W Media International, Ltd is a subsidiary of F+W Media, Inc
10151 Carver Road, Suite #200, Blue Ash, OH 45242, USA

Text and Designs © Ella Austin 2019
Layout and Photography © F&W Media International, Ltd 2019

First published in the UK and USA in 2019

A catalogue record for this book is available from the British Library.

ISBN-13: 978-1-4463-0728-1 UK paperback
SRN: R8725 UK paperback

ISBN-13: 978-1-4463-0741-0 US paperback
SRN: R9995 US paperback

ISBN-13: 978-1-4463-7722-2 PDF
SRN: R8672 PDF

ISBN-13: 978-1-4463-7721-5 EPUB
SRN: R8671 EPUB

Printed in China by RR Donnelley for:
F&W Media International, Ltd
Pynes Hill Court, Pynes Hill, Exeter, EX2 5AZ, UK

10 9 8 7 6 5 4 3 2 1

Content Director: Ame Verso
Acquisitions Editor: Sarah Callard
Managing Editor: Jeni Hennah
Project Editor: Lynne Rowe
Design Manager: Anna Wade
Design & Art Direction: Sam Staddon
Photographer: Jason Jenkins
Illustrator: Kuo Kang Chen
Production Manager: Beverley Richardson

F&W Media publishes high quality books on a wide range of subjects.
For more great book ideas visit: www.sewandso.co.uk

Layout of the digital edition of this book may vary depending on reader hardware and display settings.